Anonymous

A New Spelling Book on the Comparative Method with Side-Lights fromHistory

Fourth Edition

Anonymous

A New Spelling Book on the Comparative Method with Side-Lights fromHistory
Fourth Edition

ISBN/EAN: 9783337253219

Printed in Europe, USA, Canada, Australia, Japan

Cover: Foto ©Thomas Meinert / pixelio.de

More available books at **www.hansebooks.com**

A

NEW SPELLING BOOK

ON THE COMPARATIVE METHOD

WITH

SIDE-LIGHTS FROM HISTORY

FOURTH EDITION

LONDON
ALFRED M. HOLDEN
23 PATERNOSTER ROW, E.C.
1893

INTRODUCTION

THE difficulty of spelling—a difficulty which is felt even by able and well-educated persons—arises from the fact that the English language has never been in possession of one fixed and uniform manner of writing down the sounds of which it is composed. Every Saxon scribe wrote pretty much as he pleased, wrote as he pronounced; and a northern scribe pronounced his words very differently from a scribe in Surrey or in Kent. In early times, the English language was not one language, but a compost of several dialects. Even as late as the fourteenth century, there were in our language three well-marked dialects, each with its own grammar and its own mode of pronunciation. Each dialect had its own pronunciation; and therefore each scribe had his own way of writing down the different words. **Wold** in the north was written down **weald** in the south.

This state of things continued down to the introduction of the printing-press in 1474. If there had existed in England any corporate body with power and knowledge to revise the spelling of our speech, that body would probably have taken the opportunity given by the invention of printing to give to the printed symbols representing the spoken sounds a more self-consistent, regular, and scientific character than they had. But there was no such body; and the various ways of printing or expressing sounds to the eye were not reformed by the printing-press, but were on the contrary fixed and perpetuated even down to the present time. The English language has been called a "conglomerate of dialects." This is quite correct: but it is more;

for, in addition to the native English dialects, which had their own various ways of spelling, the language has received contributions from Danish, from Norman-French, from Latin, and, indeed, from almost every language under the sun. And each of these contributions brought its own way of spelling along with its own words. It is to the Norman-French that we owe the absurd spelling of **people** and of **view**. It is no wonder that Lord Lytton, looking on these and similar spellings of so-called English words, declared that the invention of English spelling was due to the "Father of Lies."

This irregularity and self-inconsistency fell heaviest on the vowels. This was to be expected. For the vowels are more variously pronounced by different people than the consonants, which are merely stops of the breath, or "breath-pennings," and are made by us all in a tolerably uniform manner.

Our language is said to possess thirteen different vowel-sounds; but there are 104 ways of representing these vowel-sounds to the eye.

(i) There are fourteen ways of presenting to the eye (or of printing) a long ō; as in **boat, fold, dough, toe,** etc.
(ii) There are twelve ways of printing a short ĭ; as in **sit, busy, Cyril, women,** etc.
(iii) There are twelve ways of printing a short ĕ; as in **wet, lead, any, bury,** etc.
(iv) There are ten ways of printing a long ē; as in **mete, marine, meet, meat, key, quay,** etc.
(v) There are thirteen ways of printing a short ŭ; as in **bud, love, rough, flood,** etc.
(vi) There are eleven ways of printing a long ū; as in **rude, move, blew, true,** etc.

Now it is practically impossible for the young learner to "get up" these 104 ways of writing down our vowel-sounds; what he does, and what he must do, is to learn each word as a separate and individual entity, to remember the **look** of it, and to reproduce that look when he writes it down. Thus it is almost impossible to remember in how many ways a long ī may be printed; but the learner, when he sees

wise, buys, pies, eyes, size, guise, and **sighs,** remembers each of these forms in and for itself, and reproduces them as he saw each in print. But he cannot, and he dares not, draw up for himself any general rule, or make any classification regarding the way in which a long I is or may be printed. Again, he finds a long ā represented to the eye in five different ways in **wait, weight, great, they,** and **say**; and he is compelled to remember *in each case* how that sound must be represented, and, to do this, he is obliged to regard each separate word as an individual entity, and not as subject to classification,—or as one in a series of similarly spelt words. Once more, his eye is puzzled and confused by the many different ways of printing a long ū, when he sees **issue, view, beauty, nuisance,** and **now.** Four out of these five ways are fashions derived from the French language; but this does nothing towards reconciling the learner to them. On the contrary, he is disgusted, and properly disgusted, to find that his own language, not satisfied with its own various fashions of bad and irregular spelling, goes out of its way to adopt, from other languages, newer and more irritating methods of absurd spelling.

What is the result? The result is that the learner can draw up no rules, can make no classifications, can form no habits. If he forms any mental habits at all, they are bad habits. They are the bad habits of imitating the irregularities of his ill-spelt language—irregularities which he must imitate if he is to be regarded as spelling "correctly." He learns, indeed, the bad habits of numerous Saxon and Norman-French scribes who have unwittingly laid on the shoulders of numerous generations of growing Englishmen and Englishwomen a burden not easy to be borne.

What is the cure for all this irregularity, malformation, and instability in our printed symbols? There is, for the present at least, no cure except that which is to be found in hard work and accurate observation.

To receive the printed forms of words with complete accuracy into the brain, there must be

(i) **Isolation.**

There should be

(ii) **Comparison** of contrasted forms. For example, the two forms of **ei** and **ie** may be contrasted, as in

(*a*) | receive | and | relieve |

Again, two different ways of writing (or printing) the words may be adopted, as in

(*b*) | *receive* | and | receive |

(iii) The third step is

Reproduction.

That is to say, the learner should enter in a writing-book all the words in which he has made mistakes, and should, from time to time, rewrite these words so as to accustom himself to the **look** of them. For, until we have a self-consistent and scientific mode of spelling, it is only by the EYE, and not by the reason, that we can tell whether a word has been rightly spelt. "There is now," says the Professor of Anglo-Saxon in the University of Cambridge, "only one rule—a rule which is often carefully but foolishly concealed from learners,—namely, to go entirely by the LOOK of a word, and to spell it as we have seen it spelt in books."

It follows from this that learning to spell is only a training of the eye; and, to train the eye, perpetual reproduction of words is necessary. This reproduction may be in two ways: (i) by **copying**; (ii) by **dictation**. The former requires the very smallest effort of attention; and it is quite possible for a learner to copy correctly, and yet to spell wrongly when he comes to write something of his own composition. But, when the learner has to write to dictation, his powers of memory and of accurate reproduction are called upon, and the effort of attention is very much more vigorous.

PART I
THE VOWEL-SOUNDS OF THE ENGLISH LANGUAGE

PART I.

THE VOWEL-SOUNDS OF THE ENGLISH LANGUAGE

I. THE VOWEL A.

1. The **short** sound of A is represented to the eye simply by **a,** as in **add, and,** etc.
 (i) **Contrasts:** pat, pate ; rat, rate.
 (ii) **Curiosities:** plaid, bade.

2. The **long** sound of A is generally represented by **a + e.** But it is also printed with the letters **ai, ay ; ei, ey ;** and even with **ea.**
 1. **a + e :** ate, bate, cate, pate, rate, state.
 2. **ai :** aim, bait, claim, faith, pair, stain.
 3. **ay :** bay, day, fay, gay, nay, may.
 4. **ei :** eight, heir, neighbour, rein, their, weight.
 5. **ey :** convey, hey ! obey, prey, whey, they.
 6. **ea :** bear, break, great, steak, wear.

 (i) **Contrast:** their (= belonging to them) and there (= in that place).
 (ii) **Curiosities:** gauge (measure) ; gaol (= jail) ; inveigh.

LESSON 1.

ail	bear	break	faint
aim	bait	brake	feint
ache	bare	care	fare

Lesson 2.

gaol	hail	mail	rain
gauge	frail	male	reign
gale	feint	maim	rein

Lesson 3.

saint	skein	tare	veil
scare	stake	taint	vein
share	steak	tear	weight

3. The **middle** sound of A is represented by **a**; by **au**; and also by **ea** and **e**, if before an **r**.

    1. **a**: ass, calf, half, chance, dance, grasp.
    2. **au**: aunt, draught, haunch, haunt, launch.
    3. **ea** (before **r**): heart, hearth.
    4. **e** (before **r**): Berks, clerk, Derby, sergeant.

    Curiosities: guard, quaff.

Lesson 4.

aunt	dance	guard	prance
calf	draft	haunt	sergeant
chance	grant	launch	Berks
clerk	grass	mart	Derby

4. The **broad** sound of A is represented by **a**; and also by **au** and **aw**.

    1. **a**: all, ball, call, chalk, small, tall.
    2. **au**: caught, cause, fraud, gauge, pause, taught.
    3. **aw**: brawl, crawl, claw, jaw, squaw, yawl.

    Curiosities: George, cord; squad, squash.

Lesson 5.

chalk	daub	gauze	squall
caught	fall	laws	squaw
cause	falcon	naughty	waltz
cord	fraud	pause	yawl

LESSON 6.

(Sounds and Symbols mixed).

ale	bray	gauge	reign
air	break	hail	staunch
ape	faint	haunt	swarm
aunt	falcon	neigh	taught
bait	gaol	prey	thought
brawl	heir	quaff	vein

II. THE VOWEL E.

1. The **short** sound of E is represented by e ; by ea ; and by ei and ie.

    1. e : beg, bend, egg, red, sent, went.
    2. ea : breath, breast, health, threat, wealth.
    3. ei : heifer, leisure.
    4. ie : friend.

Curiosities: jeopardy, leopard ; says, said ; bury ; any, many ; Thames ; wainscot, waistcoat.

LESSON 7.

bench	dredge	leisure	thread
bread	dreamt	mend	threat
breadth	else	meant	tread
cleanse	fledge	rent	wainscot
dead	friend	said	waistcoat
dread	heifer	says	wealth

2. The **long** sound of E is represented by e + e ; by ee ; ea ; ie ; and also by ei.

    1. e + e : cede, eke, eve, here, mete.
    2. ee : been, bleed, green, keen, seen.
    3. ea : beach, peach, feat, feast, reach, teach.
    4. ie : brief, chief, grief, mien, niece, piece.
    5. ei : ceiling ; conceive, conceit ; receive, receipt.

Curiosities: key, quay ; people ; marine, fatigue.

Lesson 8.

been	either	meet (*v*.)	sheath (*n*.)
beach	eve	meat (*n*.)	sheathe (*v*.)
breed	feat	peer	stream
breeze	free	plead	team
cede	greet	reach	wreath (*n*.)
eel	heath	reed	wreathe (*v*.)

Lesson 9.

antique	imbecile	marine	routine
caprice	intrigue	oblique	ultramarine
critique	machine	pique	verdigris
fatigue	magazine	police	unique

THE VOWEL I.

1. The **short** sound of I is represented by i simply; by i + e; by ui; by ei; and even by ie.

    1. i: bill, fill, kill, still, will.
    2. i + e: give, live.
    3. ui: build, built; guild; guilt.
    4. ei: forfeit, foreign, surfeit, counterfeit.
    5. ie: sieve, mischief.

(i) **Curiosities**: pretty; women; biscuit, circuit, conduit; carriage, marriage; parliament.

(ii) When a final syllable is not accented, the sound of its vowel, however it may be spelt, is liable to become that of a short i, as in **cabbage, vintage**; in **bargain, captain**; in **carriage, marriage**, etc. etc.

Lesson 10.

build	give	marriage	rich
built	hitch	mountain	rill
fill	kick	motive	rinse
flinch	live	pinch	stitch
forfeit	mist (*n*.)	pit	which (*pro*.)
foreign	missed (*v*.)	pretty	witch (*n*.)

2. The **long** sound of I is represented to the eye by i alone ; by the letters **i + e** ; by **y** ; by **igh** and **eigh**; by **uy** ; and **ui**.

    1. **i**: bind, find, kind, rind, wind (*v.*)
    2. **i + e**: blithe, dine, dive, five, strive, wine.
    3. **y**: by, cry, fly, try, wry ; dye.
    4. **igh** and **eigh**: high, height ; bright, light, sight.
    5. **uy**: buy, guy.
    6. **ui**: guide, guile ; guise, disguise.

    Curiosities : eye ; aisle (of a church).

LESSON 11.

bind	fife	guile	might
blithe	five	guise	right
buy	fly	high	sight
cry	flight	height	wright
crier	fry	lie	wine
dine	guide	lyre	writhe
diver			

LESSON 12.

(Sounds and Symbols mixed).

aisle	foreign	nightly	slid
aye (=yes)	guy	quire	slide
buy	line	riser	tin
cabbage	mice	risen	tithe
dye (=colour)	mine	sieve	win
eye	miss	sink	wine

THE VOWEL O.

1. The **short** sound of O is represented by **o** simply.

    1. **o**: cot, dot, hot, not ; moss, odd.

  (i) **Curiosities** (with a final e) ; copse, horse, dodge, lodge.

  (ii) **Curiosities**: knowledge ; laurel.

2. The **long** sound of O is represented in fourteen different ways. Of these the most important are : **o + e** ; **oa** ; **oe** ; **ou** ; and **ow**.
    1. **o + e** : bone, clothe, cone, hone, stone, strove.
    2. **oa** : oats, boat, coat, groat ; loaf ; soap.
    3. **oe** : doe, foe, hoe, sloe, toe.
    4. **ou** : dough, though ; mould, soul.
    5. **ow** : grow, know, low ; owe.
    (i) The letter **o** alone sometimes represents its long sound ; as in *so, lo! most, post ; folk, yolk*.
    (ii) **Curiosities** : sew, sewn ; beau, bureau ; hautboy, mauve ; yeoman, yeomanry.

LESSON 13.

blot	lop	moan (=grieve)	sot
bloater	low	pot	soar (*v.*)
blow	mop	pour	sore (*adj.*)
cot	mope	rod	sock
coat	mow	road (*n.*)	soak
dole (=a share)	mown (=cut)	rowed (*v.*)	yolk

LESSON 14.

bronze	growth	note	sod
cocoa	hoe	notary	soul
cupboard	hone	noble	sown (seed)
dodge	low	post	sewn (cloth)
foe	lone	rot	woe
groan	mould	rote	yolk

THE VOWEL U.

1. The **short** sound of U is represented to the eye by the letter **u** itself ; by **o** ; by **o + e** ; and even by **ou**.
    1. **u** : but, cut, hut, rut.
    2. **o** : son, month ; worse, worship ; comfort, company.
    3. **o + e** : done, dove, love, none.
    4. **ou** : rough, tough, young ; flourish, nourish.
    Curiosities : blood, flood ; scourge ; once ; tongue ; birth.

Lesson 15.

come	glove	none	scourge
dull	hum	nurse	some
done	judge	once	sponge
dungeon	love	pump	tongue
front	monk	purse	tough
furze	month	rough	worse

2. The **long** sound of U is represented by **u** alone; by u + e; oo; and by **ou**.

    1. **u**: bush, full, put, push.
    2. **u + e**: brute, flute; mule, mute; rude; tube.
    3. **oo**: cool, tool, stool, stood; smooth, soothe.
    4. **ou**: could, soup, should.

Curiosities: move, prove, behove; flue, glue; grew, stew; bruise, fruit, suit, recruit; do, to; shoe, canoe; through; view; ewe.

Lesson 16.

bull	flew	look	sluice
bruise	flute	lose	suit
cool	fruit	moon	through
choose	glue	new	true
could	grew	prove	yew
ewe	hue	rule	view

Lesson 17.

(Sounds and Symbols mixed).

birch	goose	new	scourge
birth	loose	none	shoe
blood	mood	once	sponge
does	moon	prove	too
fruit	month	put	tough
gun	move	rude	whose

DIPHTHONGS.

1. A **Diphthong** is a sound made by the rapid running together of two vowels, so that we seem to hear, not two vowels, but only one. Like the simple vowels, they are written down in different ways; and the EYE has to observe in which word one fashion is employed, and in which another.

2. The symbols **oi** and **oy** have the same sound, but are employed in different words. The contrast must therefore be noticed.

Lesson 18.

boil	ahoy!	avoid	moist
broil	boy	coin	soil
coil	coy	join	spoil
foil	cloy	joiner	toil
join	joy	joist	voice
joint	toy	hoist	void

Curiosities: buoy; quoit.

Lesson 19.

boy	choice	destroy	moist
boil	coil	joy	noise
buoy (a float)	coin	join	poise
broil	coy	hoist	rejoice

3. The contrast of **eu** and **ew**, and of both with **u + e**, must be carefully noted.

Lesson 20.

chew	dupe	pew	ague
dew	Europe	stew	argue
few	feud	yew	ensue
mew	mule	anew	issue
new	mute	sinew	pursue

Curiosities: beauty; lieu; view; queue.

PART II
THE INITIAL CONSONANTS OF ENGLISH WORDS

PART II

THE INITIAL CONSONANTS OF ENGLISH WORDS

Consonants at the beginning of a word are sometimes sounded in a peculiar manner—in a way different from the sound usually given to them.

1. **Ch** is sometimes sounded at the beginning (and even in the middle) of a word like **sh**, and sometimes like **k**.

LESSON 1.

sh	k	sh	k
chaise	chaos	chandelier	chameleon
champagne	chasm	chevalier	character
chagrin	chord	debauchee	Christmas
chamois	chorus	machine	chronicle
charlatan	choral	souchong	chronology

Curiosities: headache; stomach; epoch; monarch, tetrarch.

2. **Ch** is sometimes sounded at the beginning of a word like **tsh**.

LESSON 2.

chalice	chafe	chalk	chandler
chancel	chair	cheap	change
chancellor	challenge	cheese	channel
chapel	chamber	chew	chant
chaplain	champ	champion	chaplet
chest	chaff	chance	charge

Lesson 3.

chariot	chaste	chestnut	choice
chicken	chastise	chess	choose
chide	cheer	chief	cherry
chill	cherish	chimney	churn
charity	chink	chine	chocolate
charm	chirrup	chisel	cherub

3. In several words—all derived from Greek—**ch** has the sound of **k**.

Lesson 4.

character	choir	chorus	chronicle
chemist	choler	Christmas	chronometer
chimera	chord	chromatic	chrysalis

4. The initial forms **de** and **di** must be carefully distinguished. When rapidly pronounced, they sound very much the same.

Lesson 5

decant	dictate	decoy	direct
decay	didactic	deduce	diván
decease	digest	deface	diverge
deceive	digress	default	divert
decide	dilate	defer	divest
declare	dilemma	defile	divide

5. The initial forms **en** and **in** are sometimes confounded, and ought carefully to be kept apart. (**En** generally = to make; **in** = not; sometimes = in).

Lesson 6.

enable	inability	encourage	incessant
enchain	inapplicable	encumber	incite
enchant	inapt	endanger	incombustible
encircle	incapable	endear	income
enclose	incautious	endorse	incomplete
encompass	incense	endow	inculcate

Lesson 7.

enforce	infirm	enlist	injudicious
enfranchise	inflate	enliven	injustice
engrain	inflexible	ennoble	innocent
engulf	influenza	enrage	innovation
enlarge	inglorious	enrol	innumerable
enlighten	ingratitude	enthrone	insensible

NOTE.—There are several words which are spelt indifferently with an **en** or an **in**—with an **em** or **im** ; but the forms here given are generally considered the best.

Lesson 8.

encumber	imbedded
engraft	imbittered
enrol	impoverish
enslave	inquire
ensnare	insure
entreat	intrench

6. The initial forms **for** and **fore** are sometimes confused ; as they are often pronounced nearly alike.

Fore = in front of. *For* = from ; and has a negative force, as in *forbid* = to bid *not* to do.

Lesson 9.

forbear	forebode	forgive	foreknow
forbid	forecast	forlorn	forerun
forfend	foreclose	forsake	foresee
forget	foredate	forswear	foretaste

(i) **Forfend** = to defend against.
(ii) **Forlorn** = utterly lost. ('The *for* here intensifies.)
(iii) **Forsake** = to give up *seeking*.
(iv) **Forego** = to go *without*. But it has nothing to do with *fore*, and ought to be spelled **forgo**.

7. The initial form **kn** is seldom mistaken, except by the very careless. (In the last century, both consonants were always pronounced. Thus *knee* was sounded *ik-nee*.)

Lesson 10.

knack	nag	knell	Noll
knapsack	nap	knick-knack	nick
knave	nave	knife	niggard
knead	need	knight	night
knee	near	knit	net
kneel	needle	knob	noddle

(i) **Knave** was the O.E. word for *boy*.
(ii) **Kneel** is the verb from the noun *knee*.
(iii) **Knit** is the verb from the noun *knot*.

8. Careless writers have been known to confuse **pre** and **pro**. This comes from the fact that these syllables are generally not accented, and are hence rapidly pronounced.

Lesson 11.

precede	proceed	preoccupy	pronounce
predict	proclaim	prepare	propose
predominate	produce	prepay	propound
prefer	profess	prescribe	proscribe
prejudge	prolong	presént	protést
premise	promise	presume	provoke

To **prescribe** is to give directions; to **proscribe** is to outlaw, or to publish the name of a person to be punished.

9. **Per** and **pur** must be carefully distinguished.

Per = Lat. *per*, through; *pur* is a French form of the Lat. *pro*, for.

Lesson 12.

——	purblind	perfect	purpose
perceive	purchase	persecute	pursue
perchance	purloin	persecution	pursuit
percussion	purport	persuade	purvéy

(i) **Purblind** now means *partly blind;* but in former times it meant *wholly blind*. It is a contraction of *pure blind* (*pure* = *wholly*).

(ii) **Pursue** is the same Latin word as **persecute**; only it has come to us through French.

(iii) **Purvey** is only another form of the word **provide**. But **purvey** has come into our language through French, and **provide** has come direct from Latin.

10. **Sc** and **sk** require to be distinguished.

Lesson 13.

scabbard	skate	scandal	skill
scaffold	skein	scant	skim
scald	skeleton	scar	skip
scale	sketch	scarce	skirmish
scallop	skewer	scarf	skirt
scamper	skiff	scavenger	skittish

11. **Ther** and **thir** are different symbols : the first is Greek, the latter pure English. In some words **th** has the sound of **t**.

Lesson 14.

therapeutic	third	Thames
thermal	thirteen	Thomas
thermometer	thirty	thyme

(i) **Therapeutic** = relating to the art of healing. **Thermometer** = a measure of heat.

(ii) In all three derivatives from *three*, the *r* has changed its place. But, in older English, we said *thritty* for *thirty*, etc.

12. Many words have at the beginning of them a **ph** with the sound of **f**; and sometimes also in the middle. (These words come to us from the Greek language.)

Lesson 15.

phalanx	blasphemy	alphabet	pamphlet
phaeton	camphor	atmosphere	philosophy
phantom	cipher	metaphor	seraphim
pheasant	elephant	paraphrase	epitaph
phrase	emphasis	prophet	triumph
physic	ephod	sophist	trophy

13. Some words begin with an **sc**, which has the simple sound of **s**. (This **sc** generally comes before an **e** or an **i**.)

Lesson 16.

scene	sceptre	scintillate	scissors
scent	scimitar	scion	scythe

Exception : sceptic.

14. The initial form of **sch** is peculiar. It has the simple sound of **s**; or of **sk**. It has also to be carefully observed and contrasted with **sc** and **sh**.

Lesson 17.

schedule	science	shed	shingle
schism	sciatica	sheer (*adj.*)	share
		sheik (a chief)	shire
scheme		shield	shore
school		shimmer	

15. The initial form **ty** is found only in Greek words—with the exception of **typhoon** (a circular gale), which is Chinese.

Lesson 18.

tympanum (the drum of the ear)	typhoon	tyrant
type	typhus	tyro

16. The contrast between the initials **w** and **wh** is one of some importance.

Lesson 19.

wale (mark of a stroke)	whale	ween	wheeze
warp (thread in a loom)	wharf	week	whelk
weal (welfare)	wheal	weep	whelm
weasel	wheat	weevil (a small beetle)	whelp
weed	wheedle	weird (fated)	whence
		were	wherry

Lesson 20.

wet	whet (to sharpen)	windy	whimper
weather	whether (or no)	win	whin
way	whey	wine	whine
webbed	whiff	wire	whirl
wig	Whig (opposite of Tory)	wistful (eager)	whisper
wile (a trick)	while	wit	whit

PART III

WORDS OF LIKE SOUND
BUT DIFFERENT SPELLING AND MEANING

PART III

WORDS OF LIKE SOUND
BUT DIFFERENT SPELLING AND MEANING

Lesson 1.

adds, 3d person sing. of Add.
adze, a cooper's axe.
ail, to be unwell.
ale, a drink.
air, the atmosphere.
e'er, ever.
ere, before.
heir, an inheritor.
airy, open to the air.
eyry, an eagle's nest.
aisle, a passage in a church.
isle, an island.
all, every one.
awl, a shoemaker's tool.
allowed, permitted.
aloud, in a loud tone.
altar, a place set apart for sacrifice.
alter, to change.

Lesson 2.

analyst, one who analyses.
annalist, a historian.
anchor, of a ship.
anker, a liquid measure.
ant, an insect.
aunt, a female relative.
arc, part of a circle.
ark, a chest.
ascent, climbing.
assent, agreement.
eat, past tense of Eat.
eight, a number.
auger, a tool for boring.
augur, a soothsayer.
aught, anything.
ought, should.

Lesson 3.

bad, evil, wicked.
bade, past tense of Bid.
bail, surety.
bale, a bundle of merchandise.
bait, food to entice animals.
bate, to lessen, abate.
baize, a kind of cloth.
bays, plural of Bay.
bald, without hair.
bawled, past tense of Bawl.

ball, anything of a round shape.
bawl, to shout loudly.

bare, uncovered.
bear, an animal.

bark, of a dog.
barque, a kind of small ship.

Lesson 4.

baron, a lord.
barren, bare, unfruitful.

base, low, mean.
bass, the low part in music.

bay, an opening in the coast.
bey, a Turkish governor.

be, to exist.
bee, an insect.

beach, the sea-shore.
beech, a tree.

bean, a vegetable.
been, participle of Be.

beat, to strike.
beet, a vegetable.

beau, a man fond of dress.
bow, a weapon.

Lesson 5.

beer, a kind of drink.
bier, a frame on which the dead are carried.

bell, that rings.
belle, a beautiful woman.

berry, a small fruit.
bury, to put under ground.

berth, a sailor's sleeping-place.
birth, the act of being born.

bight, a small opening in the coast.
bite, to wound with the teeth.

blew, past tense of Blow.
blue, the colour.

boar, a wild beast.
bore, past tense of Bear.

board, a flat piece of wood.
bored, past tense of Bore.

boarder, one who boards in a house.
border, edge, margin.

Lesson 6.

bold, daring.
bowled, in cricket.

bolder, comparative of Bold.
boulder, a large rounded stone.

bole, the stem of a tree.
bowl, a basin.

born, given birth to.
borne, carried.
bourn, boundary, limit.

borough, a town with a corporation.
burrow, a rabbit-hole.

bough, limb of a tree.
bow, to bend.

boy, a male child.
buoy, a floating mark, over rocks, etc.

braid, a plait.
brayed, past tense of Bray.

brake, a thicket.
break, to burst or rend apart.

bread, that we eat.
bred, past tense of Breed.

Lesson 7.

brewed, past tense of Brew.
brood, offspring.

brews, 3d person sing. of Brew.
bruise, a mark caused by a blow.

bridal, a wedding.
bridle, of a horse.
Britain, the country.
Briton, a native of Britain.
broach, to pierce.
brooch, an ornament.
brows, plural of Brow.
browse, to eat tender branches.
bruit, to noise abroad.
brute, a beast.
but, conjunction, etc.
butt, a cask.
buy, to purchase.
by, preposition.
bye, a term in cricket.

Lesson 8.

calendar, an almanac.
calender, a press used in cloth-making.
candid, open, frank.
candied, covered with sugar.
cannon, a large gun.
canon, a church dignitary.
canvas, sail-cloth.
canvass, to solicit votes.
carat, a weight for gold.
carrot, a vegetable.
cask, a barrel.
casque, a helmet.
cast, to throw.
caste, rank among Hindus.
cause, reason.
caws, 3d person sing. of Caw.

Lesson 9.

cede, to yield, give up.
seed, what is sown.

ceiling, of a room.
sealing, participle of Seal.
cell, a small chamber or cave.
sell, to exchange goods for money.
cellar, a room underground.
seller, one who sells.
censer, a pan for burning incense.
censor, one who blames or censures.
cent, a hundred; a coin.
scent, a smell.
sent, participle of Send.
cereal, any kind of grain.
serial, a story, etc., published in parts.
cession, a yielding, giving up.
session, a sitting (of Parliament, etc.)

Lesson 10.

chagrin, annoyance.
shagreen, a kind of leather.
chair, a seat.
char or chare, } to do odd jobs.
chased, past tense of Chase.
chaste, pure.
cheap, not dear.
cheep, the sound made by a young bird.
check, to restrain, curb.
cheque, an order for money.
chews, 3d person sing. of Chew.
choose, to select.
choir, a body of singers.
quire, twenty-four sheets of paper.
choler, anger.
collar, an article of dress.

Lesson 11.

chord, in music.
cord, string.

cite, to summon.
sight, seeing.
site, situation.

clause, part of a sentence.
claws, plural of Claw.

climb, to mount up.
clime, climate.

coarse, not fine.
corse, another form of Corpse.
course, a running.

coarser, comparative of Coarse.
courser, a swift horse.

colonel, a military officer.
kernel, of a nut.

complement, that which completes.
compliment, a piece of civility.

Lesson 12.

core, the heart of a fruit.
corps, a body of troops.

cote, a small house (in dovecote).
coat, that we wear.

council, an assembly for consultation.
counsel, advice.

councillor, a member of a council.
counsellor, an adviser.

cousin, a relative.
cozen, to cheat.

creak, to make a harsh grating noise.
creek, a narrow inlet of water.

crewel, worsted.
cruel, savage, unkind.

Lesson 13.

crews, plural of Crew.
cruise, to sail to and fro.

cubical, shaped like a cube.
cubicle, a sleeping-place.

cue, a rod used in billiards.
queue, the tail of a wig.
Kew, a village near London.

currant, a small dried grape.
current, a stream.

cygnet, a young swan.
signet, a seal.

cymbal, a musical instrument.
symbol, a sign.

Lesson 14.

dam, a bank to confine water.
dam, mother of a sheep.

Dane, a native of Denmark.
deign, to condescend.

day, of the week.
dey, a Moorish ruler.

days, plural of Day.
daze, to dazzle.

dear, beloved, costly.
deer, an animal.

demean, to lower, make mean.
demesne, an estate.

desert, to forsake.
dessert, fruits, etc., served at the close of a meal.

deviser, one who invents or devises.
divisor, the number by which we divide.

dew, condensed vapour.
due, owing.

die, to depart from life.
dye, to colour.

Lesson 15.

dire, terrible.
dyer, one who dyes.

doe, a female deer.
dough, unbaked bread, etc.
does, plural of Doe.
doze, a light sleep.
done, participle of Do.
dun, a colour.
dost, 2d person sing. of Do.
dust, dry earth, etc.
draft, a bill of exchange.
draught, of air, water, etc.
dyeing, participle of Dye.
dying, participle of Die.

earn, to gain by labour.
urn, a vessel for water, etc.
ewe, a female sheep.
yew, a tree.
you, a personal pronoun.
ewes, plural of Ewe.
use, to make use of.
yews, plural of Yew.

Lesson 16.

fain, eager.
fane, a temple.
feign, to pretend.
faint, to swoon.
feint, a pretence.
fair, beautiful.
fare, food.
fate, destiny.
fête, a festival.
fays, plural of Fay.
phase, appearance.
feat, a remarkable deed.
feet, plural of Foot.

felloe, part of a wheel.
fellow, a companion.
ferule, a ruler.
ferrule, on a walking-stick.

Lesson 17.

filter, to strain liquids.
philtre, a love-charm.
find, to discover.
fined, past tense of Fine.
fir, a tree.
fur, of an animal.
firs, plural of Fir.
furs, plural of Fur.
furze, a prickly shrub.
flea, an insect.
flee, to run away.
flew, past tense of Fly.
flue, a chimney.
floe, a collection of floating ice.
flow, to run like water.
flour, ground wheat.
flower, a blossom.

Lesson 18.

fore, the front.
four, a number.
fort, a building for defence.
forte, that in which one excels.
forth, an adverb.
fourth, the ordinal of Four.
foul, unclean.
fowl, a bird.
frays, plural of Fray.
phrase, a form of words.
freeze, to become ice.
frieze, a coarse kind of cloth.

fungous, spongy.
fungus, a spongy plant.

Lesson 19.

gage, a pledge.
gauge, to measure.

gait, manner of walking.
gate, an entrance.

gamble, to play games of chance for money.
gambol, to frisk.

gild, to overlay with gold.
guild, a corporation.

gilt, participle of Gild.
guilt, wickedness.

grate, for a fire.
great, large.

grater, an instrument for grating nutmegs, etc.
greater, comparative of Great.

Lesson 20.

grays, things of a gray colour.
graze, to feed on grass.

grease, soft fat.
Greece, the country.

greaves, armour for the legs.
grieves, 3d person sing. of Grieve.

grisly, hideous, horrible.
grizzly, of a gray colour.

groan, a deep sigh.
grown, participle of Grow.

grocer, one who sells tea, etc.
grosser, comparative of Gross.

guessed, past tense of Guess.
guest, a visitor.

Lesson 21.

hail, frozen rain.
hale, healthy.

hair, of the head.
hare, an animal.

hall, a large room.
haul, to drag.

handsome, of fine appearance.
hansom, a vehicle.

hart, a stag.
heart, an organ of the body.

hay, dried grass.
hey! an exclamation.

heal, to cure.
heel, of the foot.

hear, to perceive by the ear.
here, in this place.

Lesson 22.

heard, past tense of Hear.
herd, a collection of cattle.

hew, to cut.
hue, colour.
Hugh, a man's name.

hide, to conceal.
hied, past tense of Hie.

hie, to hasten.
high, lofty.

higher, comparative of High.
hire, wages.

him, objective case of He.
hymn, a sacred song.

ho! an exclamation.
hoe, a tool.

Lesson 23.

hoard, a hidden store.
horde, a wandering tribe.

hoarse, having a harsh voice.
horse, an animal.
hoes, plural of Hoe.
hose, stockings.
hole, a hollow place.
whole, complete.
holy, sacred.
wholly, entirely.
hoop, a ring of wood or metal.
whoop, a loud shout.
hour, of the day.
our, belonging to us.

Lesson 24.

idle, unemployed.
idol, an image.
in, a preposition.
inn, a tavern.
indict, to accuse.
indite, to write.

jam, preserved fruit.
jamb, the side-post of a door, etc.

key, of a lock.
quay, a wharf.
kill, to put to death.
kiln, a large drying-oven.
knave, a rascal.
nave, of a church.

Lesson 25.

knead, to work dough.
need, to want.
knew, past tense of Know.
new, fresh, recent.

knight, a title of rank.
night, the time of darkness.
knot, a tie.
not, a word of denial.
know, to be acquainted with.
no, a word of denial.
knows, 3d person sing. of Know.
nose, the organ of smell.

Lesson 26.

lac, a kind of gum.
lack, to be in want of.
lacks, 3d person sing. of Lack.
lax, not strict.
lade, to load.
laid, past tense of Lay.
lain, participle of Lie.
lane, a narrow road.
lair, the abode of a wild beast.
layer, a bed or stratum.
laps, plural of Lap.
lapse, to slip.
lea, a meadow.
lee, the side on which the wind does not blow.

Lesson 27.

lead, a metal.
led, past tense of Lead.
leaf, of a tree.
lief, willingly.
leak, to let water in or out.
leek, a kind of onion.
leant, past tense of Lean.
lent, past tense of Lend.
lessen, to make less.
lesson, something read or learnt.

liar, one who speaks falsely.
lyre, a musical instrument.
lie, to recline.
lye, a mixture of ashes and water.

Lesson 28.

lightening, participle of Lighten.
lightning, the electric flash.
limb, a member (of the body).
limn, to paint.
links, of a chain.
lynx, a wild animal.
literal, according to the letter.
littoral, belonging to the sea-shore.
lo! an exclamation.
low, not high.
load, a burden.
lode, a vein of mineral ore.
lowed, past tense of Low.
loan, something lent.
lone, lonely.

Lesson 29.

maid, a girl.
made, past tense of Make.
mail, for letters.
male, of sex.
main, chief, principal.
mane, of a horse.
maize, Indian corn.
maze, a labyrinth.
manor, an estate.
manner, method.
mantel, the shelf above a fireplace
mantle, a cloak.
mare, a female horse.
mayor, a civic dignitary.

mark, a sign made with a pencil, etc. (also a German coin.)
marque, "letters of marque" gave leave to merchantmen to act as men-of-war.
marshal, a high military officer.
martial, warlike.

Lesson 30.

mead, a meadow.
meed, a reward.
mean, low, base.
mien, air, look.
meat, food.
meet, to encounter.
mete, to measure.
medal, a decoration for bravery, etc.
meddle, to interfere.
meddler, one who meddles.
medlar, a kind of fruit.
metal, iron, etc.
mettle, spirit, courage.
mewl, to cry like a baby.
mule, an animal.
mews, a stable.
muse, to meditate.
might, strength, power.
mite, a small insect.

Lesson 31.

miner, a worker in a mine.
minor, a person below the age of twenty-one.
missed, past tense of Miss.
mist, watery vapour.
moan, a low sound of pain.
mown, participle of Mow.
moat, a trench round a castle.
mote, a small speck.

mode, manner.
mowed, past tense of Mow.
morning, the early part of the day.
mourning, grieving.
muscle, of the body.
mussel, a kind of shell-fish.
mustard, a pungent plant.
mustered, past tense of Muster.

nay, no.
neigh, a sound made by a horse.
none, not one.
nun, an inmate of a nunnery.

Lesson 32.

O ! or
oh ! } an interjection.
owe, to be indebted.

oar, for rowing.
o'er, a short form of Over.
ore, unrefined metal.
ode, a kind of poem.
owed, past tense of Owe.

one, a number.
won, past tense of Win.

pail, a vessel for water, etc.
pale, white, wan.

pain, suffering.
pane, of glass.

pair, a couple.
pare, to cut off rind.
pear, a fruit.

palate, the roof of the mouth.
palette, for mixing painters' colours on.
pallet, a small bed.

Lesson 33.

pause, to stop for a while.
paws, plural of Paw.

peace, rest.
piece, a part, portion.

peak, a pointed top.
pique, to wound the pride.

peal, of bells.
peel, the skin or rind of fruit.

pearl, a jewel.
purl, a drink.

pedal, a lever worked by the foot.
peddle, to sell as a pedlar does.

peer, an equal, a nobleman.
pier, a projecting quay.

pendant, a hanging ornament.
pendent, hanging (adjective).

Lesson 34.

plaice, a kind of fish.
place, locality.

plaid, a kind of shawl.
played, past tense of Play.

plain, a level piece of country.
plane, a carpenter's tool.

plait, to interweave.
plate, a flat dish.

pleas, plural of Plea.
please, to give pleasure.

plum, a kind of fruit.
plumb, a leaden weight.

pole, a long staff.
poll, the number of votes in an election.

pore, a small passage in the skin.
pour, to cause to flow.

Lesson 35.

practice, noun.
practise, verb.
praise, to commend.
prays, 3d person sing. of Pray.
pray, to supplicate.
prey, what is seized, booty.
pride, self-esteem.
pried, past tense of Pry.
pries, 3d person sing. of Pry.
prize, a reward.
principal, chief.
principle, a rule.
profit, gain.
prophet, a foreteller.
psalter, a book of psalms.
salter, comparative of Salt.
puny, very small.
puisne, a kind of judge.

Lesson 36.

quarts, plural of Quart.
quartz, a mineral.

rack, an instrument of torture.
wrack, sea-weed cast up on shore.
rain, from the clouds.
reign, to rule.
rein, for driving.
raise, to lift up.
rays, plural of Ray.
raze, to lay level with the ground.
rap, to strike sharply.
wrap, to enfold.
rapped, past tense of Rap.
rapt, enraptured.
wrapped, past tense of Wrap.

read, to peruse.
reed, a kind of jointed grass.
read, past tense of Read.
red, a colour.

Lesson 37.

reck, to consider.
wreck, destruction of a ship.
reek, to steam or smoke.
wreak, to inflict vengeance.
rest, quiet.
wrest, to twist away by force.
rhyme, in verse.
rime, hoar-frost.
right, correct, just.
rite, a ceremony.
wright, a workman.
write, to form letters with a pen or pencil.
ring, to sound like a bell.
wring, to twist.
road, an open way.
rode, past tense of Ride.
rowed, past tense of Row.
roe, eggs of a fish.
row, a line, rank.

Lesson 38.

roes, plural of Roe.
rose, a flower.
rows, plural of Row.
rood, one-fourth of an acre.
rude, uncultivated, rough.
root, of a plant.
route, a line of march, direction.
rote, frequent repetition.
wrote, past tense of Write.
rough, uneven.
ruff, an article of dress.

rues, 3d person sing. of Rue.
ruse, a trick, stratagem.
rung, past tense of Ring.
wrung, past tense of Wring.
rye, a kind of grain.
wry, twisted.

Lesson 39.

sail, of a ship.
sale, the operation of selling.
sailer, a sailing-vessel.
sailor, a seaman.
scar, a mark left by a wound.
scaur, a cliff.
scene, a view or sight.
seen, participle of See.
scull, a small light oar.
skull, the head.
sea, a part of the ocean.
see, to perceive with the eyes.
seam, the line made by sewing.
seem, to appear.
sear, to dry up.
sere, dried up, withered.

Lesson 40.

seas, plural of Sea.
sees, 3d person sing. of See.
seize, to take violent hold of.
senior, elder.
signor, Italian for Sir.
serf, a slave attached to the soil.
surf, of the sea.
serge, a kind of cloth.
surge, the swelling of a large wave.
sew, to work with needle and thread.
sow, to put seed in the ground.
so, adverb and conjunction.

shear, to cut or clip.
sheer, pure, unmingled.
sighed, past tense of Sigh.
side, the edge or border.
sighs, 3d person sing. of Sigh.
size, extent.

Lesson 41.

sign, a mark or token.
sine, a term in trigonometry.
slay, to kill.
sleigh, a carriage with runners instead of wheels.
sleight, cunning, dexterity.
slight, small, slender.
sloe, a wild plum.
slow, not fast.
soar, to rise high in the air.
sore, painful.
soared, past tense of Soar.
sword, a weapon.
sold, past tense of Sell.
soled, furnished with a sole.
sole, of the foot or the boot.
soul, the spirit.

Lesson 42.

some, part of the whole.
sum, an amount.
son, a male child.
sun, the source of light and heat.
staid, grave, sober.
stayed, past tense of Stay.
stair, a flight of steps.
stare, to gaze fixedly.
stake, a strong pointed stick.
steak, a slice of meat.

stationary, standing still.
stationery, a stationer's goods.
steal, to take by theft.
steel, hardened iron.
step, a pace.
steppe, a vast uncultivated plain.

tern, a kind of sea-bird.
turn, to move round.
their, belonging to them.
there, in that place.
threw, past tense of Throw.
through, from end to end.

Lesson 43.

stile, steps for climbing a fence.
style, manner, method.
storey, in a house.
story, a tale, narrative.
straight, direct, not crooked.
strait, a narrow sea-passage.
subtler, comparative of Subtle.
sutler, a camp-follower.
succour, aid.
sucker, a young shoot.
suite, a retinue.
sweet, like sugar.

tacked, shifted her course (of a ship).
tact, delicate skill.
tacks, plural of Tack.
tax, money levied by the State.

Lesson 44.

tail, of an animal.
tale, a story.
tare, a wild plant.
tear, to rend.
team, a yoke of horses, etc.
teem, to abound.
tear, water from the eyes.
tier, a row.
teas, different kinds of tea.
tease, to annoy.

Lesson 45.

throe, a sensation of agony.
throw, to fling.
throne, a royal seat.
thrown, participle of Throw.
thyme, a scented herb.
time, season, period of duration.
tide, the ebb and flow of the sea.
tied, past tense of Tie.
to, towards, etc.
too, also, overmuch.
two, twice one.
toe, of the foot.
tow, coarse flax or hemp.
told, past tense of Tell.
tolled, past tense of Toll.
ton, twenty hundredweight avoirdupois.
tun, four hogsheads of wine.

Lesson 46.

tracked, past tense of Track.
tract, a region, a short treatise.
trait, a feature.
tray, for carrying cups, etc.
travail, heavy labour or pain.
travel, to journey.
treaties, plural of Treaty.
treatise, a formal essay.

vain, useless, empty.
vane, a weathercock.
vein, a blood-vessel.
vale, a valley.
veil, a covering for the face.
vial, a small glass vessel.
viol, an old musical instrument.

Lesson 47.

wade, to walk in water.
weighed, past tense of Weigh.
wail, to lament aloud.
wale, the raised mark left by a cut from a whip, etc.
wain, a waggon.
wane, to grow less.
waist, the middle of the body.
waste, to consume uselessly.
wait, to remain.
weight, heaviness.

waive, to dispense with.
wave, of the sea.
ware, merchandise.
wear, to consume by use.

Lesson 48.

way, road, manner.
weigh, to find the weight of.
weak, feeble.
week, seven days.
weald, an open upland.
wield, to handle.
wean, to separate.
ween, to think, suppose.
weather, state of the atmosphere.
wether, a sheep.
wood, a collection of trees.
would, auxiliary verb.

yolk, of an egg.
yoke, for oxen, etc.

PART IV
WORDS THAT MAY BE CONFOUNDED

PART IV

WORDS THAT MAY BE CONFOUNDED

Lesson 1.

absolute, complete, unlimited.
obsolete, no longer in use.

accede, to agree to.
exceed, to go beyond, surpass.

accept, to receive willingly.
except, to leave out, exclude.

access, approach.
excess, something beyond what is needed or desired.

accidence, a part of grammar.
accidents, plural of Accident.

adapt, to make apt or fit.
adept, one who is skilled in a particular pursuit.

addition, the process of adding.
edition, of a book.

Lesson 2.

adherence, steady attachment.
adherents, plural of Adherent.

advice, noun.
advise, verb.

affect, to influence.
effect, to accomplish.

alder, a tree that grows near water.
elder, a tree with purple berries.

alimentary, pertaining to food.
elementary, primary.

allay, to quiet.
alley, a narrow passage.
alloy, to mix fine metal with base.
ally, one who makes an alliance.

allude, to refer indirectly.
elude, to escape by stratagem from.

Lesson 3.

allusion, an indirect reference.
illusion, a deceptive appearance.

alms, gifts of charity.
arms, plural of Arm.

antic, an odd trick.
antique, ancient.

apposite, suitable.
opposite, over against, contrary.

assay, to test metal ore.
essay, to attempt.

assistance, aid.
assistants, plural of Assistant.

attendance, the act of waiting upon.
attendants, plural of Attendant.

Lesson 4.

balm, soothing ointment.
barm, yeast.

bath, noun.
bathe, verb.

breaches, plural of Breach.
breeches, trousers.

breath, noun.
breathe, verb.

capital, the chief or most important thing.
capitol, the temple of Jupiter at Rome.
champaign, an open level country.
champagne, a light sparkling wine.
choose, present tense.
chose, past tense.

Lesson 5.

choral, belonging to a choir.
coral, a hard, coloured substance
cloth, noun.
clothe, verb.
collision, a violent striking together.
collusion, a secret agreement to deceive.
command, to order.
commend, to put into the hands of, intrust to.
complacent, pleased, gratified.
complaisant, desiring to please.
concert, agreement, a musical entertainment.
consort, a partner, companion.
condemn, to declare guilty, to sentence.
contemn, to despise.

Lesson 6.

confidant, } a friend intrusted with secrets.
fem. confidante
confident, positive, believing firmly.

copula, a bond, a conjunction.
cupola, a dome.

corporal, relating to the body.
corporeal, having a body, material.

corps, a body of troops, etc.
corpse, a dead body.

correspondence, an interchange of letters.
correspondents, plural of Correspondent.

courtesy, good manners.
curtsey, a sign of respect made by a woman.

critic, one who criticises.
critique, a critical article.

Lesson 7.

dairy, a place where milk is kept.
diary, a daily record of events.
decease, death.
disease, illness.
decry, to depreciate, cry down.
descry, to perceive at a distance.
deference, respectful submission.
difference, what distinguishes one thing from another.
demur, to hesitate, to object.
demure, affectedly quiet or modest.
deprecate, to pray that a thing may not happen.
depreciate, to undervalue, disparage.
descent, act of descending.
dissent, difference of opinion.

Lesson 8.

device, noun.
devise, verb.

discomfit, to disconcert, balk.
discomfort, uneasiness.
divers, several (in number).
diverse, different (in kind).
dragon, a fabulous monster.
dragoon, a kind of soldier.

eclipse, of the sun or moon.
ellipse, an oval figure.
elicit, to entice, draw out.
illicit, unlawful.
eligible, fit to be chosen.
illegible, unreadable, indistinct.
emigrant, one who migrates *from* a country.
immigrant, one who migrates *to* a country.

LESSON 9.

eminent, distinguished.
imminent, threatening, close at hand.
emit, to throw or give out.
omit, to leave out.
empire, the dominion of an emperor.
umpire, one who is appointed to decide disputes.
envelop, verb.
envelope, noun.
errand, a going on a message.
errant, constantly wandering or erring.
eruption, a breaking *out*.
irruption, a breaking *in*.
exaltation, state of being exalted.
exultation, triumphant joy.
exercise, to train by practice.
exorcise, to expel an evil spirit.
extant, still standing or existing.
extent, the space to which a thing extends.

LESSON 10.

factitious, artificial, unnatural.
fictitious, imaginary.
fisher, one who catches fish.
fissure, a crack, crevice.

genius, a special inborn gift.
genus, kind; a group of species.
genteel, fastidiously refined.
gentile, one who is not a Jew.
gentle, mild, amiable.
glacier, a river of ice.
glazier, one who glazes, or puts in window-panes.
gorilla, the largest kind of monkey.
guerilla, one of a band of Spanish irregular troops.
grisly, hideous, horrible.
gristly, consisting of gristle.
grizzly, of a gray colour.

LESSON 11.

harrow, a farming implement.
harry, to plunder and destroy.
human, belonging to the race of men.
humane, kindly, merciful.

idle, lazy, inactive.
idol, an image that is worshipped.
idyl, a short poem, pastoral or narrative.
impassable, not to be passed.
impassible, incapable of feeling.
impostor, one who imposes upon people.
imposture, the act of imposing upon people.
impotent, powerless, feeble.
impudent, shameless, insolent.

38 WORDS THAT MAY BE CONFOUNDED

ingenious, skilful, clever.
ingenuous, noble, honourable.
insight, thorough knowledge.
incite, to stir up, urge on.
interpellation, an interruption.
interpolation, a word or passage inserted in a book, etc., by another hand.

Lesson 12.

jalap, an unpleasant medicine.
julep, a sweet, pleasant liquor.

lath, a thin slip of wood.
lathe, a machine for turning and shaping wood, etc.
least, superlative of Little.
lest, for fear that (a conjunction).
levee, a reception of visitors.
levy, a raising of money or troops.
lichen, a plant growing on rocks and trees.
liken, to make like.
lineament, a feature.
liniment, a kind of ointment.
liqueur, a flavoured drink, a cordial.
liquor, anything liquid.
loth, adjective.
loathe, verb.
loose, free, unbound, not tight.
lose, to part with, be deprived of.

Lesson 13.

magnate, an important dignitary.
magnet, a substance that attracts iron or steel.

message, a communication sent from one person to another.
messuage, a dwelling-house with grounds attached.,
minister, a servant; a clergyman.
minster, a cathedral church.
missal, the Roman Catholic mass-book.
missile, a weapon that is thrown.
monetary, relating to money.
monitory, giving warning.

ordinance, something ordained, a decree.
ordnance, great guns, artillery.

Lesson 14.

patience, power of enduring.
patients, plural of Patient.
patron, a protector, helper.
pattern, an example, model.
pelisse, a kind of ladies' garment.
police, a body of men who guard public order and safety.
pistil, of a flower.
pistol, a weapon.
perspective, the art of drawing objects as they appear to the eye.
prospective, relating to the future.
picket, an outpost.
piquet, a game at cards.
plaintiff, the accuser in a law-suit.
plaintive, complaining, sad.

Lesson 15.

poplar, a tall slender tree.
popular, pleasing to the people.
populace, the common people.
populous, full of inhabitants.

precede, to go before, or in front of.
proceed, to go forward.
precedent, a previous case that serves as a model.
president, one who presides.
preposition, one of the parts of speech.
proposition, something proposed.
presence, state of being present.
presents, gifts.
prophecy, noun.
prophesy, verb.

Lesson 16.

radish, an edible root.
reddish, somewhat red.
real, actually existing, genuine.
reel, to roll about as if drunk.
receipt, a written acknowledgment of something received.
recipe, a prescription; instructions for preparing food.
recourse, a seeking for aid or consolation.
resource, a contrivance.
referee, one to whom a dispute is referred.
reverie, a day-dream.
regime, form of government.
regimen, regulation of diet and habits.
regiment, a body of troops, commanded by a colonel.
rout, to defeat utterly.
route, line of march, plan of journey.

Lesson 17.

sanatory, healing, curing.
sanitary, tending to promote health.

satire, ridicule directed against vice or folly.
satyr, a sylvan deity.
sear, to dry up, wither.
seer, a prophet.
sere, dry, withered.
secret, adjective.
secrete, verb.
series, a set of things of similar kind.
serious, solemn, earnest.
sheath, noun.
sheathe, verb.
singeing, present participle of Singe.
singing, present participle of Sing.
sooth, truth.
soothe, to please with soft words.

Lesson 18.

spacious, large, roomy.
specious, plausible, apparently good.
species, a kind or variety.
statue, a carved or chiselled image.
stature, bodily height.
statute, a written law.
suit, a series or set; an action at law.
suite, a retinue, train of followers; a set of apartments.
surplice, a white clerical robe.
surplus, something left over.
swath, a line of grass, etc., cut by a scythe.
swathe, to wrap in bandages.

talents, natural gifts.
talons, claws.
thorough, adjective.
through, preposition.

tongs, for lifting coals, etc.
thongs, strips of leather for fastening anything.
track, a mark left in walking, etc.
tract, a short paper on a subject; or a piece of country.

Lesson 19.

valet, a man-servant who attends on his master's person.
valley, a hollow among hills.

venal, willing to be bribed, corrupt.
venial, pardonable, trifling.

veracity, truthfulness.
voracity, fierceness of appetite.

vertex, the top or summit.
vortex, a whirlpool.

whether, which of two?
whither, to what place.

whirl, to spin round rapidly.
whorl, a turn of the spire in a spiral sea-shell.

wreath, noun.
wreathe, verb.

PART V

CONTRASTED ENDINGS
ACCENTED

PART V

CONTRASTED ENDINGS

I
ACCENTED

Lesson 1.

1 (a). ay, eigh,   ey

affray	dismay	stray	convey
array	display		grey
betray	mislay		obey
decay	portray	inveigh	prey
defray	pray	neigh	purvey
delay	relay	weigh	survey

Lesson 2.

1 (b). ade,   aid, ayed

ambuscade	degrade	afraid
arcade	esplanade	braid
barricade	lemonade	laid
blockade	masquerade	plaid
brigade	palisade	raid
brocade	parade	upbraid
cascade	persuade	
cavalcade	pervade	
cockade	promenade	decayed
crusade	serenade	frayed

Lesson 3.

1 (c). ale,　　　　　　　　　ail

female	nightingale	assail	frail
gale	regale	avail	retail
impale	scale	curtail	quail
inhale	whale	detail	trail

1 (d). ame,　　　　　　　　　aim

became	inflame	aim
blame	selfsame	claim
defame	shame	maim
frame	surname	proclaim

Lesson 4.

1 (e). ane, ain, ein,　　　　　　　aign, eign

bane	abstain	refrain	arraign
crane	complain	regain	campaign
humane	disdain	restrain	
inane	domain		
insane	legerdemain		deign
membrane	obtain	rein	feign
profane	ordain	skein	reign

Lesson 5.

1 (f). are, air, eir,　　　　　　　ear, ere

aware	affair	bugbear
beware	corsair	forbear
compare	debonair	pear
declare	despair	swear
nightmare	repair	tear
prepare	stair	
scare		
snare		ere
square	heir	there
stare	their	where

Lesson 6.

1 (g). ase,   ace

abase	chase	disgrace	embrace
case	erase	efface	retrace

1 (h). ate, ait,   aight, eight

abate	ornate	await	straight
create	relate	bait	
debate	sedate	gait	
elate	skate	plait	eight
estate	translate	strait	freight
innate	vacate	wait	weight

Lesson 7.

1 (i). aze, ase,   aize, aise

amaze	haze	baize
blaze	maze	maize
craze	raze	
daze		
gaze		chaise
glaze	phase	praise
graze	phrase	raise

Lesson 8.

2 (a). awl, aul,   al, all

awl	haul	gall
bawl	maul	hall
brawl		pall
crawl		small
drawl	appal	squall
scrawl	enthral	stall
sprawl	jackal	thrall
yawl	withal	wall

Lesson 9.

2 (b). **aught**,   **ought**

caught	besought	ought
distraught	bought	sought
fraught	brought	thought
taught	nought	wrought

Lesson 10.

3 (a). **ed**,   **ead**

bred	behead	lead (*n.*)
fled	bread	read (*pret.*)
shed	dead	spread
shred	dread	thread
sped	instead	tread

Lesson 11.

3 (b). **el**,   **ell**

compel	bell	pell-mell
excel	cell	sell
expel	dell	shell
hotel	farewell	smell
propel	fell	spell
rebel	knell	swell

Lesson 12.

3 (c). **ense**,   **ence**

condense	commence
dense	fence
expense	hence
immense	offence
recompense	pence
sense	thence
tense	whence

Lesson 13.

4 (a). ee,

absentee
agree
assignee
chimpanzee
decree
degree
devotee
flee
free
fusee
glee
guarantee

knee
lee
legatee
lessee
mortgagee
oversee
pedigree
referee
refugee
repartee
thee
trustee

ea, ey, ay

flea
lea
pea
plea
sea
tea

———

key

———

quay

Lesson 14.

4 (b). ede,

accede
cede
centipede
concede
impede
intercede
precede
recede
secede
supersede

eed, ead

agreed
bleed
breed
exceed
greed
indeed
proceed
reed
speed
steed

succeed
weed

———

bead
knead
mead
mislead
plead
read (*pres.*)

Lesson 15.

4 (c). eef, eaf,

beef
reef

———

leaf
sheaf

ief

belief
brief
chief
grief
relief
thief

Lesson 16.

4 (d). eke, eek, iek,

		eak, ique	
eke	reek	creak	wreak
	seek	freak	
	sleek	sneak	
cheek	week	speak	antique
creek		squeak	critique
leek		streak	oblique
meek	shriek	weak	pique

Lesson 17.

4 (e). eel,

		eal	
eel	kneel	appeal	repeal
feel	peel	cochineal	reveal
genteel	reel	conceal	squeal
heel	steel	congeal	steal
keel	wheel	heal	zeal

Lesson 18.

4 (f). eme, eem, eam

eme	eem	eam	
blaspheme	deem	beam	scream
extreme	esteem	cream	seam
scheme	redeem	dream	steam
supreme	seem	gleam	stream
theme	teem	ream	team

Lesson 19.

4 (g). ene, een, ine

ene	een	ine
contravene	between	brigantine
convene	canteen	chlorine
intervene	careen	crinoline
scene	fifteen	fascine
serene	green	gelatine
	keen	glycerine

Lesson 20.

ean,	een,	ine
clean	queen	machine
dean	screen	magazine
demean	seen	marine
glean	sheen	routine
wean	spleen	sardine
	tureen	tambourine

Lesson 21.

4 (h). eep,		eap
creep	sleep	cheap
deep	steep	heap
keep	sweep	leap
sheep	weep	reap

Lesson 22.

4 (i). ere,	eer,	ear,	ier
adhere	auctioneer	appear	bombardier
atmosphere	career	arrear	brigadier
austere	charioteer	blear	cashier
cohere	domineer	clear	cavalier
hemisphere	engineer	drear	chandelier
here	gazetteer	endear	chevalier
interfere	mountaineer	gear	croupier

Lesson 23.

mere	musketeer	hear	cuirassier
persevere	mutineer	near	financier
revere	pioneer	rear	frontier
sere	privateer	smear	fusilier
severe	sheer	spear	gondolier
sincere	veneer	tear	grenadier
sphere	volunteer	year	tier

E

Lesson 24.

4 (j). ease, eace,	eese, eece, iece, is
cease	geese
crease	
decease	
decrease	fleece
grease	
increase	
lease	niece
release	piece
peace	verdigris

Lesson 25.

4 (k). ete,	eet,	eat, eit
athlete	beet	bleat
compete	discreet	defeat
complete	fleet	entreat
concrete	greet	repeat
delete	meet	retreat
effete	sheet	
mete	sleet	
obsolete	street	conceit
secrete	sweet	deceit

Lesson 26.

4 (l). eve, eeve, eave,	ieve, eive
eve	achieve
	believe
	grieve
sleeve	relieve
	reprieve
	retrieve
bereave	thieve
cleave	
greave	
heave	deceive
leave	perceive
weave	receive

LESSON 27.

4 (m). eeze, ieze, eize,	ese, eese, ease
breeze	these
freeze	
sneeze	
squeeze	cheese
wheeze	
	appease
frieze	disease
	ease
	please
seize	tease

LESSON 28.

5. il,		ill	
distil	chill	grill	skill
instil	drill	quill	thrill
until	frill	shrill	till

LESSON 29.

6 (a). ine,		ign
asinine	iodine	assign
brine	saline	benign
canine	saturnine	condign
celandine	serpentine	consign
decline	shrine	design
define	turpentine	ensign
divine	underline	malign
eglantine	valentine	sign

LESSON 30.

6 (b). ise,	ice	
concise	advice	sacrifice
merchandise	device	splice
paradise	entice	suffice
precise	price	twice

Lesson 31.

6 (c). ite,		ight, eight	
anchorite	parasite	bight	plight
anthracite	polite	blight	right
bite	quite	bright	sight
cite	recite	delight	slight
excite	requite	fight	tight

Lesson 32.

expedite	smite	flight	wight
ignite	sprite	fright	wright
incite	trite	knight	
indite	unite	light	
invite	white	might	height
mite	write	night	sleight

Lesson 33.

6 (d). ize,		ise	
assize	agonise	moralise	scandalise
prize	apologise	organise	stigmatise
size	civilise	particularise	tantalise

Lesson 34.

7 (a). oe,	ow,		ough, o
doe	below	outgrow	dough
foe	bestow	overflow	though
hoe	blow	overthrow	
sloe	crow	show	
toe	glow	slow	forego
woe	know	snow	hullo!

Lesson 35.

7 (b). ode,		oad	
abode	forebode	goad	
code	incommode	load	
corrode	mode	road	
explode	ode	toad	

ACCENTED 53

Lesson 36.

7 (c). oke,

awoke
broke
choke
invoke
joke
smoke
stroke
yoke

oak, olk

cloak
croak
oak
soak

---

folk
yolk

Lesson 37.

7 (d). ol, ole,

		oll,	oal, owl
control	condole	droll	coal
enrol	console	poll	foal
patrol	dole	roll	goal
	hole	scroll	shoal
	parole	stroll	
bole	stole	toll	
cajole	whole	troll	bowl

Lesson 38.

7 (e). ome,

chrome
dome
gnome

hippodrome
home
tome

oam

foam
loam
roam

Lesson 39.

7 (f). one, oan,

			own
alone	drone	zone	blown
atone	ozone		flown
bone	postpone		grown
condone	prone	groan	known
cone	stone	loan	own
crone	throne	moan	shown
depone	tone	roan	sown

Lesson 40.

7 (g). ore, oar,   or, oor, our

adore	lore	swore	abhor
before	moidore	yore	
bore	pore		
claymore	restore		door
deplore	score	boar	floor
encore	shore	hoar	
explore	snore	oar	
gore	sore	roar	four
ignore	store	soar	pour

Lesson 41.

7 (h). orse, oarse, ourse,   orce, ource

corse	coarse	divorce
endorse	hoarse	force
gorse		
horse		
Norse	discourse	resource
remorse	recourse	source

Lesson 42.

7 (i). ote,   oat

denote	quote	bloat	goat
devote	remote	boat	groat
dote	rote	coat	moat
mote	smote	float	stoat
promote	wrote	gloat	throat

Lesson 43.

8. our,   ower

devour	our	bower	power
flour	scour	cower	shower
hour	sour	dower	tower

ACCENTED 55

Lesson 44.

9 (a). ur,	urr, er,	err, ir, irr
blur	burr	err
cur	purr	
demur		
fur		fir
incur	confer	stir
occur	deter	
slur	inter	
spur	refer	whirr

Lesson 45.

9 (b). urn,	ern,	earn, ourn
burn	concern	earn
churn	discern	learn
return	fern	yearn
spurn	stern	
turn	subaltern	
urn	tern	adjourn

Lesson 46.

9 (c). urse, orse,	erse, earse	
curse	averse	terse
disburse	disperse	transverse
nurse	diverse	verse
purse	immerse	
	intersperse	
	perverse	hearse
worse	reverse	rehearse

Lesson 47.

10 (a). ue,	ew	
blue	crew	screw
clue	curlew	shrew
cue	dew	strew
due	drew	threw
endue	eschew	yew
flue	few	

Lesson 48.

10 (a). ue,	ew,	iew, ieu
glue	flew	view
hue	knew	
imbue	hew	
rue	mew	adieu
subdue	new	lieu
true	pew	

Lesson 49.

10 (b). use,		uce, euce	
abuse (*n.*)	obtuse	conduce	truce
abstruse	profuse	induce	
diffuse (*adj.*)	recluse	produce (*v.*)	
excuse (*n.*)	use (*n.*)	spruce	deuce

Lesson 50.

10 (c). ute,			uit
acute	dispute	minute (*adj.*)	bruit
astute	execute	mute	fruit
brute	flute	pollute	pursuit
commute	jute	refute	recruit
dilute	lute	salute	suit

PART VI
CONTRASTED ENDINGS
UNACCENTED
WITH
SILENT LETTERS

PART VI

CONTRASTED ENDINGS

II
UNACCENTED

Lesson 1.

1. age,   ege, ige, idge

advantage	manage	college
appendage	marriage	privilege
average	message	sacrilege
cabbage	mortgage	
carriage	passage	
disparage	pilgrimage	vestige

Lesson 2.

equipage	plumage	cartridge
foliage	sausage	partridge
haemorrhage	savage	porridge
language	vicarage	
luggage	vintage	

Lesson 3.

2. al,   el,   le

accidental	angel	angle
acquittal	apparel	apostle
avowal	cancel	baffle
bridal	chapel	beadle
cannibal	charnel	beetle
carnival	chisel	bible
cathedral	citadel	bottle
corporal	counsel	bridle
criminal	cudgel	candle
cymbal	dishevel	castle

Lesson 4.

al,	el,	le
diagonal	duel	couple
disposal	enamel	cradle
eternal	flannel	cripple
final	gospel	dazzle
frugal	hazel	disable
gradual	hovel	disciple
hospital	infidel	embezzle
legal	jewel	feeble
longitudinal	kennel	gentle
loyal	label	humble

Lesson 5.

marshal	level	hurdle
medal	libel	idle
menial	mackerel	marble
metal	model	meddle
mortal	morsel	myrtle
national	parcel	needle
naval	rebel	pebble
offal	satchel	people
original	scoundrel	principle
pedestal	sentinel	rifle

Lesson 6.

penal	sequel	scribble
principal	shovel	stable
prodigal	shrivel	straggle
recital	spaniel	stubble
rehearsal	tassel	thimble
rival	trammel	thistle
sandal	travel	title
triumphal	tunnel	treble
victual	vessel	trouble
vital	vowel	vegetable

Lesson 7.

3. able,   ible

abominable	irreconcilable	accessible	incorruptible
acceptable	irrevocable	audible	indefensible
admirable	lamentable	combustible	indestructible
advisable	laughable	compatible	inexhaustible
affable	manageable	comprehensible	inexpressible
agreeable	movable	contemptible	intelligible
allowable	notable	convertible	irascible

Lesson 8.

amicable	palatable	credible	irresistible
attainable	passable	digestible	legible
available	payable	discernible	perceptible
capable	peaceable	divisible	permissible
conceivable	probable	edible	possible
deplorable	reasonable	eligible	reprehensible
durable	remarkable	fallible	responsible

Lesson 9.

formidable	respectable	feasible	risible
honourable	tolerable	flexible	sensible
impenetrable	unsearchable	forcible	susceptible
implacable	unsuitable	horrible	tangible
indefatigable	valuable	incontrovertible	terrible
inevitable	vegetable	incorrigible	visible

Lesson 10.

4. cal,   cle,   ckle

chemical	medical	article	buckle
critical	monarchical	barnacle	cackle
cylindrical	musical	bicycle	cockle
cynical	nautical	binnacle	fickle
demoniacal	periodical	carbuncle	freckle
ducal	pharmaceutical	chronicle	honeysuckle
ecclesiastical	physical	circle	knuckle

Lesson 11.

cal,		cle,	ckle, kle
economical	poetical	conventicle	pickle
geographical	practical	icicle	speckle
geological	radical	manacle	tackle
geometrical	rascal	miracle	trickle
grammatical	reciprocal	obstacle	
historical	satirical	oracle	
hysterical	sceptical	pinnacle	ankle

Lesson 12.

identical	symbolical	receptacle	periwinkle
local	technical	spectacle	rankle
lyrical	tropical	tabernacle	sparkle
magical	tyrannical	treacle	sprinkle
mathematical	vertical	uncle	tinkle
mechanical	whimsical	vehicle	wrinkle

Lesson 13.

5. cial,	sial,	tial
beneficial	controversial	partial
commercial		penitential
facial		pestilential
glacial	essential	potential
judicial	influential	providential
provincial	initial	prudential
social	martial	reverential
special	nuptial	substantial

Lesson 14.

6. il,		ile	
anvil	lentil	agile	futile
April	nostril	camomile	hostile
cavil	pencil	docile	imbecile
civil	peril	domicile	missile
codicil	pupil	ductile	mobile

Lesson 15.

il,		ile	
daffodil	tendril	facile	profile
devil	tranquil	febrile	sterile
evil	utensil	fertile	textile
fossil	vigil	fragile	versatile

Lesson 16.

7. om, ome,		um	
atom	phantom	album	millennium
axiom	random	aquarium	modicum
besom	seldom	asylum	museum
blossom	symptom	conundrum	oakum
bosom	venom	decorum	odium

Lesson 17.

bottom	wisdom	delirium	opium
buxom		elysium	pendulum
custom		emporium	petroleum
earldom	income	encomium	pomatum
fathom	irksome	geranium	premium

Lesson 18.

freedom	quarrelsome	gypsum	quorum
hansom	troublesome	harmonium	rostrum
idiom	wearisome	interregnum	trapezium
kingdom	welcome	laburnum	vacuum
martyrdom	wholesome	medium	vellum

Lesson 19.

8. ain,	in,	ine
captain	assassin	destine
certain	coffin	determine
chamberlain	florin	discipline
chaplain	goblin	doctrine
chieftain	javelin	engine
curtain	muslin	ermine

Lesson 20.

ain,	in,	ine
fountain	napkin	famine
mountain	origin	heroine
murrain	satin	imagine
plantain	urchin	medicine
porcelain	vermin	rapine
villain	virgin	sanguine

Lesson 21.

9. en, in,   on

barren	ripen	apron	lesson
bedizen	risen	bacon	mason
brazen	siren	baron	myrmidon
brethren	stricken	beacon	pardon
burden	sudden	beckon	poison

Lesson 22.

enliven	threaten	blazon	prison
garden	vixen	cauldron	reckon
hyphen	warden	cotton	saffron
kitten	weaken	crimson	siphon
lengthen		damson	squadron

Lesson 23.

lessen	basin	deacon	treason
lichen	cousin	environ	unison
liken	raisin	garrison	venison
madden	rosin	glutton	waggon
patten		guerdon	weapon

Lesson 24.

10. ian,   ion

antediluvian	historian	battalion	medallion
barbarian	librarian	bunion	oblivion
Christian	meridian	carrion	opinion
civilian	plebeian	centurion	postillion

Lesson 25.

ian,   **ion**

comedian	presbyterian	champion	rebellion
cornelian	quotidian	clarion	scorpion
fustian	ruffian	criterion	scullion
guardian	tragedian	dominion	vermilion

Lesson 26.

11. geon,   **gian, gion**

bludgeon	collegian
dudgeon	theologian
dungeon	
gudgeon	
pigeon	contagion
sturgeon	legion
surgeon	region
widgeon	religion

Lesson 27.

12. cian, sion,   **tion**

academician	confession	abolition	devotion
arithmetician	convulsion	action	discretion
electrician	declension	affection	emotion
Grecian	dimension	affliction	exception
logician	excursion	anticipation	exhibition

Lesson 28.

magician	expansion	assertion	extortion
mathematician	extension	attention	fiction
musician	immersion	auction	mention
optician	mansion	caution	multiplication
patrician	mission	completion	objection

Lesson 29.

physician	oppression	concoction	option
politician	passion	congregation	persecution
rhetorician	pension	conjunction	portion
	possession	construction	redemption
	pretension	consumption	reduction

F

Lesson 30.

sion,		tion	
apprehension	procession	contradiction	reflection
ascension	session	contribution	sanction
aspersion	tension	conversation	satisfaction
compulsion	transgression	corruption	situation
concussion	version	description	subtraction

Lesson 31.

13. ar,	er,	or,	our, re
altar	adventurer	actor	armour
angular	astronomer	ambassador	behaviour
beggar	barrister	ancestor	clamour
calendar	believer	anchor	colour
caterpillar	chamber	author	demeanour
cedar	chronicler	bachelor	endeavour
cellar	chronometer	chancellor	favour
circular	collier	conqueror	fervour

Lesson 32.

collar	composer	conspirator	harbour
dollar	decanter	creator	honour
exemplar	deliver	creditor	humour
familiar	dowager	debtor	labour
friar	embroider	doctor	neighbour
globular	exchequer	governor	odour
grammar	fiddler	horror	parlour
insular	fishmonger	inferior	splendour

Lesson 33.

linear	gaoler	inspector	succour
lunar	geographer	inventor	vapour
medlar	gossamer	legislator	vigour
mortar	idolater	liquor	
muscular	inquirer	metaphor	acre
particular	interpreter	mirror	centre
peculiar	invader	orator	fibre
perpendicular	ledger	pallor	

Lesson 34.

ar,	er,	or,	re
pillar	milliner	preceptor	lustre
polar	minister	professor	manœuvre
poplar	monster	proprietor	massacre
popular	murderer	prosecutor	meagre
scholar	officer	razor	mediocre
scimitar	passenger	sailor	metre
similar	pawnbroker	sculptor	mitre
singular	photographer	solicitor	ochre

Lesson 35.

solar	prisoner	squalor	ogre
sugar	saucer	successor	reconnoitre
tabular	surrender	suitor	sabre
tartar	swimmer	surveyor	saltpetre
templar	tiger	tenor	sceptre
vicar	undertaker	traitor	sepulchre
vinegar	waiter	tutor	spectre
vulgar	weaver	warrior	theatre

Lesson 36.

14. ice,		is,	is and -ise
accomplice	justice	amanuensis	marquis
apprentice	lattice	analysis	metropolis
armistice	liquorice	antithesis	paralysis
artifice	malice	axis	portcullis
avarice	notice	basis	proboscis
benefice	orifice	chrysalis	tennis
bodice	poultice	clematis	thesis

Lesson 37.

chalice	practice (*n.*)	crisis	trellis
coppice	precipice	dais	
cowardice	prejudice	emphasis	
crevice	pumice	genesis	anise
dentifrice	service	gratis	practise (*v.*)
edifice	solstice	hypothesis	promise
jaundice	surplice	iris	treatise

Lesson 38.

15. **ous** (an adjective-suffix),   **us** (a noun-suffix)

adventurous	marvellous	apparatus
ambiguous	momentous	asparagus
analogous	monotonous	census
anomalous	monstrous	chorus
anonymous	multitudinous	circus

Lesson 39.

arduous	nervous	colossus
barbarous	ominous	convolvulus
blasphemous	perilous	crocus
chivalrous	poisonous	exodus
conspicuous	pompous	focus

Lesson 40.

covetous	posthumous	fungus
credulous	ravenous	genus
desirous	ridiculous	grampus
disastrous	riotous	hiatus
enormous	scrupulous	ignoramus

Lesson 41.

fabulous	solicitous	impetus
frivolous	sonorous	incubus
grievous	sumptuous	isthmus
hazardous	tremendous	narcissus
infamous	troublous	nautilus

Lesson 42.

jealous	tyrannous	rhombus
joyous	venomous	sarcophagus
ludicrous	villainous	surplus
lustrous	voluminous	syllabus
magnanimous	wondrous	walrus

Lesson 43.

16. eous, ious (adjective-suffixes), **eus, ius** (noun-suffixes)

aqueous	abstemious	odious
beauteous	anxious	perfidious
bounteous	bilious	precarious
contemporaneous	calumnious	rebellious
courteous	ceremonious	salubrious
erroneous	copious	serious
heterogeneous	curious	studious
hideous	delirious	tedious

Lesson 44.

igneous	dubious	various
instantaneous	fastidious	
nauseous	ignominious	
piteous	impious	nucleus
plenteous	industrious	
righteous	melodious	
simultaneous	meritorious	genius
spontaneous	obvious	radius

17. geous,   **gious**

advantageous	gorgeous	contagious	religious
courageous	outrageous	litigious	sacrilegious

Lesson 45.

18. cious,   **tious**

atrocious	officious	ambitious
audacious	pernicious	captious
avaricious	pertinacious	cautious
capacious	precious	conscientious
conscious	precocious	facetious
efficacious	sagacious	infectious

Lesson 46.

cious,		tious
ferocious	spacious	ostentatious
gracious	specious	pretentious
judicious	suspicious	propitious
loquacious	tenacious	seditious
luscious	vicious	superstitious
malicious	vivacious	vexatious

Lesson 47.

19. erous,

		orous	
boisterous	onerous	amorous	rancorous
cadaverous	ponderous	decorous	rigorous
dangerous	preposterous	dolorous	timorous
generous	prosperous	humorous	traitorous
murderous	slanderous	odorous	valorous
numerous	treacherous	omnivorous	vigorous

Lesson 48.

20. ance,

		ence
acceptance	hindrance	audience
admittance	inheritance	cadence
allegiance	insurance	circumference
alliance	nuisance	condolence
ambulance	ordinance	conference
annoyance	ordnance	conscience
appearance	penance	credence
balance	performance	essence
continuance	perseverance	experience
contrivance	resemblance	independence

Lesson 49.

conveyance	resistance	influence
countenance	riddance	interference
deliverance	severance	licence
disturbance	substance	occurrence
encumbrance	sufferance	precedence
endurance	sustenance	preference
entrance	temperance	reminiscence
forbearance	utterance	science
grievance	variance	sentence
guidance	vengeance	sequence

Lesson 50.

21. it,

		ite, uit
bandit	implicit	composite
benefit	inherit	definite
bowsprit	limit	exquisite
comfit	merit	favourite
credit	orbit	granite
cubit	plaudit	hypocrite
culprit	profit	infinite
decrepit	prohibit	opposite

Lesson 51.

discomfit	pulpit	perquisite
elicit	rabbit	requisite
exhibit	solicit	respite
exit	spirit	
explicit	summit	
habit	tacit	biscuit
hermit	transit	circuit
illicit	visit	conduit

Lesson 52.

22. ant, ent

abundant	important	accident	penitent
ascendant	intolerant	adjacent	permanent
assailant	merchant	agent	pestilent
assistant	miscreant	ancient	precedent
buoyant	occupant	apparent	predicament
compliant	pageant	client	prudent
consonant	peasant	competent	raiment
covenant	radiant	continent	recent
currant	relevant	convalescent	recumbent
defendant	remnant	correspondent	regiment

Lesson 53.

dependant (*n.*)	repentant	current	resident
descendant	sergeant	dependent (*adj.*)	reverent
discordant	significant	eloquent	serpent

Lesson 53—*continued.*

ant,		ent	
elegant	stagnant	fluent	sufficient
elephant	suppliant	indulgent	superintendent
extravagant	supplicant	magnificent	transient
flagrant	tenant	obedient	turbulent
fragrant	triumphant	omnipotent	urgent
gallant	truant	opponent	vehement
ignorant	vacant	patient	violent

Lesson 54.

23. ement,   iment

complement	accompaniment	liniment
element	compliment	merriment
implement	detriment	nutriment
increment	experiment	regiment
tenement	habiliment	rudiment
vehement	impediment	sentiment

Lesson 55.

24. y,   ey

apathy	humbly	alley
astronomy	idly	attorney
brandy	idolatry	barley
bully	infamy	chimney
canopy	jolly	cockney
chalky	larceny	covey
clergy	litany	donkey
colloquy	mahogany	galley
comedy	majesty	hackney

Lesson 56.

cruelly	marshy	honey
dusky	melancholy	jersey
early	melody	jockey
ebony	monarchy	journey
effigy	monopoly	kidney
elegy	mutiny	lackey
envy	nobly	lamprey
feebly	plaguy	medley
filthy	possibly	money

Lesson 57.

y,		ey
galaxy	probably	monkey
gently	puppy	motley
gentry	shady	parley
geography	study	parsley
geology	subsidy	pulley
geometry	treasury	turkey
grisly	trophy	valley
holy	wily	volley

Lesson 58.

25. cy,   sy

agency	juicy	apostasy	grassy
curacy	legacy	argosy	heresy
decency	policy	controversy	hypocrisy
delicacy	racy	courtesy	idiosyncrasy
despondency	saucy	dropsy	jealousy

Lesson 59.

efficacy	secrecy	embassy	leprosy
fallacy	supremacy	epilepsy	mossy
fancy	tenancy	fantasy	pleurisy
icy	tendency	gipsy	poesy
idiocy	vacancy	glossy	tipsy

Lesson 60.

26. sy,   zy

busy	flimsy	breezy
clumsy	noisy	dizzy
cosy	palsy	frenzy
daisy	pansy	hazy
drowsy	posy	lazy
easy	rosy	oozy

Lesson 61.

27. ary,

adversary
antiquary
apothecary
arbitrary
auxiliary
boundary
burglary
contrary

ery,

archery
artillery
bribery
butchery
celery
cemetery
chancery
colliery

ory

compulsory
conciliatory
congratulatory
conservatory
consolatory
contradictory
cursory
dedicatory

Lesson 62.

corollary
customary
diary
dictionary
dispensary
elementary
estuary
exemplary

cookery
deanery
debauchery
discovery
drapery
drollery
drudgery
effrontery

defamatory
deprecatory
derogatory
desultory
dilatory
factory
history
inflammatory

Lesson 63.

February
fragmentary
granary
hereditary
honorary
infirmary
library
literary

embroidery
emery
flattery
forgery
gallery
grocery
livery
lottery

interrogatory
introductory
inventory
ivory
laboratory
lavatory
memory
observatory

Lesson 64.

mercenary
missionary
necessary
ordinary
parliamentary
pecuniary
penitentiary
salary

machinery
millinery
misery
mockery
monastery
mummery
mystery
nunnery

offertory
oratory
peremptory
pillory
predatory
prefatory
preparatory
priory

Lesson 65.

ary,	ery,	ory
sanctuary	popery	promissory
secondary	raillery	promontory
secretary	scenery	purgatory
sedentary	slavery	rectory
solitary	slippery	refractory
summary	surgery	repository
vocabulary	treachery	transitory
voluntary	trumpery	victory

Lesson 66.

28. ety,		ity
anxiety	activity	iniquity
contrariety	alacrity	insanity
dubiety	authority	laity
ebriety	calamity	levity
gaiety	charity	majority
moiety	civility	perplexity
nicety	commodity	popularity
notoriety	credulity	quantity
piety	deity	reality
propriety	dignity	security
rickety	enmity	serenity
satiety	eternity	solemnity
sobriety	fertility	timidity
society	gravity	vanity
variety	ingenuity	vicinity

Lesson 67.

29. city,		sity	
atrocity	mendacity	adversity	intensity
audacity	paucity	animosity	monstrosity
authenticity	rapacity	curiosity	necessity
capacity	sagacity	density	obesity
duplicity	scarcity	diversity	perversity
eccentricity	simplicity	falsity	pomposity
electricity	velocity	generosity	propensity
felicity	vivacity	immensity	university
ferocity	voracity	impetuosity	verbosity

SILENT LETTERS

Lesson 68.

a : caoutchouc, extraordinary.

b : bomb, catacomb, climb, comb, crumb, debt, doubt, dumb, hecatomb, indebted, jamb, lamb, limb, numb, plumber, redoubt, redoubtable, subtle, succumb, thumb, tomb.

Lesson 69.

c : czar, indict, victuals.

ch : drachm, schism, yacht.

ck : blackguard.

d : groundsel, handkerchief, handsel, handsome.

e : height, luncheon, puncheon, scutcheon, sleight, truncheon.

Note.—e after c or g (as in dungeon, pageant, peaceable, serviceable, vengeance, etc.) need not be regarded as a silent letter, since it has the function of softening the consonant.

Lesson 70.

g : apophthegm, arraign, assign, benign, campaign, champagne, champaign, condign, consign, deign, design, diaphragm, ensign, feign, foreign, gnarl, gnash, gnat, gnaw, gnome, gnomon, gnu, impugn, malign, paradigm, phlegm, poignant, reign, resign, seignior, sign, sovereign.

SILENT LETTERS

LESSON 71.

gh : although, aught, besought, bight, blight, borough, bough, bought, bright, brought, caught, daughter, delight, distraught, dough, doughty, drought, eight, fight, flight, fought, fraught, freight, fright, furlough, haughty, height, high.

LESSON 72.

Inveigh, knight, light, might, naughty, neigh, neighbour, nigh, night, nought, ought, plight, plough, right, sigh, sight, slaughter, sleigh, sleight, slight, slough, sought, straight, taught, thigh, thorough, though, thought, through, tight, weigh, weight, wight, wright, wrought.

LESSON 73.

h : aghast, catarrh, dahlia, diarrhœa, dishabille, ghastly, gherkin, ghost, hæmorrhage, heir, honest, honorarium, honorary, honour, honourable, hour, myrrh, rhapsody, rhetoric, rheumatism, rhinoceros, rhododendron, rhombus, rhubarb, rhyme, shepherd, thyme.

LESSON 74.

i : business, carriage, friend, marriage, parliament, puisne.

k : knack, knapsack, knave, knead, knee, kneel, knell, knelt, knew, knick-knack, knife, knight, knit, knob, knock, knoll, knot, knout, know, knowledge, knuckle, unknown.

LESSON 75.

l : almond, alms, balk, balm, behalf, calf, calm, calve, caulk, chalk, could, folk, half, halve, palm, psalm, qualm, salmon, salve, should, stalk, talk, walk, would, yolk.

lf : halfpenny.

m : mnemonics.

n : autumn, column, condemn, contemn, damn, hymn, kiln, limn, solemn.

Lesson 76.

p : pneumatic, pneumonia, psalm, psalter, pseudonym, pshaw, psychology, ptarmigan,˙raspberry, receipt, sempstress.

Note.—p between m and t is practically silent, as in assumption, attempt, consumption, contempt, empty, exempt, impromptu, peremptory, presumptuous, prompt, redemption, resumption, sumptuous, symptom, tempt.

Lesson 77.

ph : apophthegm, phthisis.

ps : corps.

s : aisle, demesne, island, isle, puisne (*pronounced* puny), viscount.

t : apostle, boatswain, bouquet, bustle, castle, chasten, chestnut, christen, Christendom, Christmas, croquet, epistle, fasten, glisten, gristle, hasten, jostle, listen, mistletoe, moisten, mortgage, nestle, often, ostler, pestle, ragout, rustle, soften, surtout, thistle, throstle, trait, waistcoat, whistle, wrestle.

Note.—t before ch is practically silent, as in catch, blotch, hutch, witch, wretch, etc.

Lesson 78.

u : aunt, beguile, biscuit, blackguard, bouquet, build, buy, circuit, conduit, conquer, coquette, croquet, disguise, etiquette, gauge, guarantee, guard, guardian, guerdon, guerilla, guess, guest, guide, guild, guildhall, guile, guillotine, guilt, guinea, guise, guitar, laugh, liquor, masquerade, mosquito, piquant, piquet, quay, queue, quoit, roguery, roguish, victuals.

Lesson 79.

w : answer, awry, boatswain, cockswain, gunwale, housewife, sword, who, whole, wholesome, whoop, whooping-cough, wrack, wrangle, wrap, wrath, wreak, wreath, wreck, wren, wrench, wrest, wrestle, wretch, wretched, wriggle, wright, wring, wrinkle, wrist, writ, write, writhe, written, wrong, wrote, wroth, wrought, wrung, wry.

Lesson 80.

1. The Premier was arraigned for high treason, and consigned to the Tower. 2. Throughout the campaign, the leader never deigned to give any explanation of his designs. 3. The Honourable Mr. Gwynne talked for more than an hour with the heir-apparent. 4. The knight well knew that behind the knoll an ambush was hidden. 5. I should like to borrow a halfpenny stamp on behalf of a friend. 6. Deer-stalking and salmon-fishing were the holiday pursuits of this member of parliament. 7. The Mistletoe Bough is a tale told in rhyme. 8. The fall of the leaves in autumn is a solemn sight. 9. I guarantee that you will not repent of having given a guinea for that guitar. 10. Last night the ghost of the czar appeared to her, with a knapsack on its back, and a silk handkerchief over its head.

Lesson 81.

1. Their neighbour, the honest shepherd, had all the symptoms of rheumatic fever. 2. Near the castle grew a clump of chestnut trees, in the shape of a rhombus. 3. A handsome yacht had just weighed anchor and was slowly making her way out of the bight. 4. This roguish coquette disguises her thoughts so well that the guardsman fancies her in love with him. 5. He drew a whistle from his waistcoat pocket. 6. The marriage of the plumber's daughter was as yet unknown to her friends. 7. As he knelt on one knee

before the shrine, straightway a marvellous light shone upon him. 8. Although he besought the sovereign to spare his life, he was condemned for his share in the attempt to wreck the Stuart dynasty. 9. The wreath which she wore at the masquerade was made of dahlias. 10. She taught her sons as well as her daughters to knit, and the boys caught the knack of it almost as soon as the girls.

Lesson 82.

1. Some of the passengers began to feel qualms before the boat left the quay. 2. No honorary member shall be allowed to take part in the business. 3. If the Guards could have stormed the heights, there would have been no doubt of our victory. 4. Turkey rhubarb and tincture of myrrh are drugs. 5. The paper devoted several columns to the viscount's career. 6. He wrenched the sword from his hand and ran him through the body; watching him as he writhed in agony. 7. I am going to buy an island, several miles in circuit, and build a house upon it. 8. Rhododendrons might be planted beside the walks and near the quoiting-ground. 9. The Epistle to the Romans was written by the Apostle Paul. 10. His fingers and thumbs were quite benumbed by the extraordinary cold. 11. He wrote a receipt for the money.

PART VII

CONTRASTED DERIVATIVES

PART VII

CONTRASTED DERIVATIVES

Lesson 1.		Lesson 3.		Lesson 5.	
abolish	abolition	apathy	apathetic	assail	assault
abound	abundant	aperient	aperture	Atlas	Atlantic
abstain	abstinent	apology	apologetic	attend	attention
accede	access	apostate	apostasy		attentive
acclaim	acclamation	appeal	appellation	authority	authoritative
acquire	acquisition	appear	apparent	avert	averse
actor	actress		apparition		aversion
adhere	adhesion	appertain	appurtenance	balsam	balm
	adhesive	applaud	applause	beast	bestial
admit	admission	apply	application	behave	behaviour

Lesson 2.		Lesson 4.		Lesson 6.	
admit	admissible	apprehend	apprehension	behove	behoof
admonish	admonition	approve	approbation	believe	belief
	admonitory	aristocrat	aristocracy	benefit	benefactor
adolescent	adult	armour	armorial	bequeathe	bequest
advise	advice		armory	bereave	bereft
allude	allusion	aroma	aromatic	beseech	besought
analyse	analytic	article	articulate	bitumen	bituminous
angle	angular	ascend	ascension	brass	brazen
animus	animosity		ascent		brazier
anxious	anxiety	ascribe	ascription	brief	brevity

CONTRASTED DERIVATIVES

Lesson 7.		Lesson 10.		Lesson 13.	
brief	abbreviate	clamour	clamorous	congeal	congelation
Britain	British	cleave	cleft	consanguineous	consan-
	Briton	cleric	clergy		guinity
broad	breadth	coal	collier	conscience	conscientious
brother	brethren	coalesce	coalition	consequence	consequen-
burgh	burgess	cock	coxcomb		tial
candle	chandelier	cohere	cohesion	constable	constabulary
	chandler		cohesive	consume	consumption
car	chariot	collide	collision	contagion	contagious
cartilage	cartilaginous	column	colonnade	contain	continent

Lesson 8.		Lesson 11.		Lesson 14.	
castle	castellated	commit	commission	contain	content
cataleptic	catalepsy		commissary	contemn	contempt
catechise	catechumen		commissariat	contend	contention
caution	cautious	common	community	controvert	controversy
cease	cessation		communion	convert	converse
	incessant		communicate		conversion
cede	cession	compel	compulsion	convoke	convocation
chancellor	chancery		compulsory	corrode	corrosion
chapel	chaplain	compendium	compen-	courteous	courtesy
chevalier	chivalry		dious		curtsey

Lesson 9.		Lesson 12.		Lesson 15.	
chevalier	chivalrous	compound	component	credence	credentials
choir	choral	comprehend	compre-	creed	credence, etc.
	chorister		hension	crime	criminal
choose	chose	concede	concession	cross	crosier
	choice	conceive	conceit		crusade
Christian	Christendom		conception	curious	curiosity
cicatrix	cicatrise	conclude	conclusion	dame	damsel
cinder	cinerary	condescend	condescen-		madam
circumstance	circum-		sion	decay	decadence
	stantial	confidence	confidential	deceive	deceit

CONTRASTED DERIVATIVES

Lesson 16.
deceive	deception
decide	decision
declaim	declamation
decline	declension
deduce	deduction
deep	depth
defend	defence
	defensive
deference	deferential
delirium	delirious

Lesson 17.
delude	delusion
democrat	democracy
demolish	demolition
denounce	denunciation
deride	derision
descend	descent
describe	description
despair	desperate
despise	despicable
destroy	destruction

Lesson 18.
detain	detention
devise	device
die	dying
diminish	diminution
dine	dinner
disapprove	disapproba-tion
disbelieve	disbelief
discolour	discoloration
discourteous	discourtesy

Lesson 19.
discreet	discretion
disobey	disobedient
	disobedience
disprove	disproof
dissemble	dissimulation
dissent	dissension
dissolve	dissolute
dissuade	dissuasion
dissyllable	dissyllabic
distant	distance

Lesson 20.
distend	distention
distinguish	distinct
divert	diversion
divide	division
dolour	dolorous
dumb	dummy
dyspepsia	dyspeptic
eat	ate
eclipse	ecliptic
ecstasy	ecstatic

Lesson 21.
eight	eighth
ellipse	elliptical
embassy	ambassador
emit	emissary
emperor	empress
emphasis	emphatic
empire	imperial
enemy	enmity
	inimical
enter	entrance

Lesson 22.
enter	entry
envy	invidious
epilepsy	epileptic
equinox	equinoctial
essence	essential
esteem	estimable
evade	evasion
evolve	evolution
example	exemplary
	exemplify

Lesson 23.
exceed	excess
exclaim	exclamation
exclude	exclusion
expand	expansion
expel	expulsion
expend	expense
explain	explanation
explode	explosion
expound	exponent
extend	extension

Lesson 24.
extend	extent
extinguish	extinct
feast	festal
feign	feint
fever	febrile
finish	finite
five	fifth
	fifteen
	fifty
fire	fiery

CONTRASTED DERIVATIVES

Lesson 25.
fledge	fledgeling	goose	gosling	ingenious	ingenuity
flower	flourish	grain	granary	inquire	inquisition
	floral	grass	graze	inscribe	inscription
	florin	Greece	Greek	intend	intense
	florist		Grecian		intent
fly	flight	grieve	grief		intention
foil (as in trefoil)	foliage	gross	grocer	intercede	intercession
	folio	half	halve	intermit	intermission
fool	folly	harbour	harbinger	intervene	intervention
forbid	forbade	heir	hereditary	intrude	intrusion

Lesson 26.

Lesson 29.

Lesson 32.

forbear	forbore	heir	heritage	invade	invasion
foresee	foresight	heresy	heretic	invert	inverse
forth	further	high	height		inversion
four	forty	honour	honorary	inveigh	invective
fourteen	fortnight	humble	humility	invoke	invocation
frank	franchise	hunger	hungry	joke	jocose
freeze	frozen	hypocrite	hypocrisy		jocular
furnish	furniture	hypothesis	hypothetical		jocund
genteel	gentility	idiot	idiocy	judge	judicial
gentle	gentry	impel	impulse		judicious

Lesson 27.

Lesson 30.

Lesson 33.

genus	generic	impetuous	impetuosity	judge	judicature
	generous	impious	impiety	join	junction
geometer	geometry	imply	implicit		juncture
	geometrician	impose	impostor	labour	laborious
giant	gigantic	include	inclusive		laboratory
gird	girth	index	indices	late	latter
give	gift		indicate	lay	laid
glass	glaze	indiscreet	indiscretion	lead	led
gloss	gloze	inflame	inflammable	leaf	leaves
gluten	glutinous	infringe	infraction	leprous	leprosy

CONTRASTED DERIVATIVES

Lesson 34.
licence	licentiate
	licentious
lie	lying
lighten	lightning
long	length
loose	lose
	lost
	loss
lunacy	lunatic
machine	mechanical

Lesson 35.
maintain	maintenance
marquis	marchioness
mask	masquerade
matter	material
merchant	merchandise
	mercantile
message	messenger
metal	metallic
miscellaneous	miscellany

Lesson 36.
mischief	mischievous
misconceive	misconception
mislay	mislaid
mislead	misled
mispronounce	mispronunciation
mood	modify
	modulate
money	monetary

Lesson 37.
monosyllable	monosyllabic
monstrous	monstrosity
motley	mottled
nine	ninth
nose	nostril
notorious	notoriety
nourish	nurse
	nurture
	nutriment

Lesson 38.
novice	novitiate
number	numerical
	numerous
obey	obeisance
	obedient
	obedience
obtrude	obtrusion
	obtrusive
occur	occurrence
odium	odious

Lesson 39.
odour	odorous
offend	offence
	offensive
omen	ominous
omit	omission
one	only
opaque	opacity
opium	opiate
opprobrium	opprobrious
ordain	ordinance

Lesson 40.
ordain	ordinary
	ordnance
palace	palatial
panorama	panoramic
paralysis	paralytic
parenthesis	parenthetic
parish	parochial
parley	parliament
	parlour
	parlance

Lesson 41.
part	partake (=part+take)
	parcel
participle	participial
pass	pastime
passage	passenger
paste	pastry
pasture	pastern
pathos	pathetic
pauper	poverty

Lesson 42.
pave	pavior
pay	paid
peddle	pedlar
penitence	penitential
	penitentiary
penny	pence
people	popular
	population
	populace
	populous

CONTRASTED DERIVATIVES

Lesson 43.
perceive	perception
permit	permission
persuade	persuasion
pertain	pertinent
pervade	pervasive
pervert	perverse
pestilence	pestilential
•Peter	petrel
Pharisee	pharisaical
pharmacy	pharmaceutical

Lesson 44.
Philip	philippic
piano	pianist
picture	pictorial
pious	piety
pillar	pillory
pinch	pincers
pity	piteous
plenty	plenteous
plumb	plummet
polish	polite

Lesson 45.
pompous	pomposity
Pope	papal
pork	porcupine
	porpoise
porridge	porringer
portend	portent
Portugal	Portuguese
practise	practice
	practitioner
precipice	precipitous

Lesson 46.
preconceive	preconception
preface	prefatory
prejudge	prejudice
prescribe	prescription
presume	presumption
	presumptuous
pretend	pretence
	pretension
	pretentious

Lesson 47.
prevail	prevalent
	prevalence
price	precious
prime	primrose
	primogeniture
	premier
proceed	procedure
	process
proclaim	proclamation
produce	production

Lesson 48.
profound	profundity
promise	promissory
pronoun	pronominal
pronounce	pronunciation
propel	propulsion
prophesy	prophecy
propose	proposition
prorogue	prorogation
proscribe	proscription

Lesson 49.
prose	prosaic
protrude	protrusion
provide	provision
	proviso
providence	providential
provoke	provocation
prudence	prudential
psalm	psalter
publish	publication
pursue	pursuit

Lesson 50.
pursue	pursuant
radish	radical
rancour	rancorous
recede	recess
receive	recipe
	recipient
	receipt
	reception
	receptacle
reclaim	reclamation

Lesson 51.
recognise	recognition
reconnoitre	reconnaissance
recover	recuperative
redeem	redemption
redouble	reduplication
redound	redundant
reduce	reduction
reflect	reflex
relieve	relief

CONTRASTED DERIVATIVES

Lesson 52.

remain	remnant
remit	remiss
renounce	renunciation
repair	reparation
	irreparable
repel	repulse
reprehend	reprehensible
reprove	reproof
	reprobate
require	requisite

Lesson 53.

require	request
resolve	resolute
resound	resonant
respond	response
restore	restaurant
resume	resumption
retain	retention
	retinue
retrograde	retrogression
reveal	revelation

Lesson 54.

reverence	reverential
revert	reverse
	reversion
revoke	revocation
	irrevocable
revolve	revolution
	revolt
rhombus	rhomboid
rigour	rigorous
rite	ritual

Lesson 55.

romance	romantic
Sabbath	Sabbatical
	Sabbatarian
satisfy	satisfaction
Saturn	Saturday
save	Saviour
scarf	scarves
scathe	scathless
school	scholar
	scholastic

Lesson 56.

science	scientific
scribe	scribble
	Scripture
	scrivener
scurf	scurvy
secede	secession
seclude	seclusion
secret	secrecy
seam	sempstress
seethe	sodden

Lesson 57.

self	selves
sentence	sententious
Septuagint	septuagenarian
serf	servile
	servant
	servitude
series	serial
sever	separate
sheaf	sheaves

Lesson 58.

sheep	shepherd
shelf	shelves
	shelving
side	sidle
sieve	sift
simile	semblance
	simulate
site	situation
slow	sloth
solve	solution

Lesson 59.

soluble	solubility
speak	spake
	spoke
	speech
species	special
	specify
	specific
spill	spilt
spleen	splenetic
stay	staid

Lesson 60.

stimulus	stimulant
strategy	stratagem
strive	strife
strong	strength
submit	submission
subscribe	subscription
substance	substantial
subvert	subversion
succeed	success
sunder	sundry

CONTRASTED DERIVATIVES

Lesson 61.		Lesson 63.		Lesson 65.	
superficies	superficial	tinge	tint	viceroy	viceregal
superscribe	superscription	trace	track	vigour	vigorous
superstition	superstitious	tragic	tragedy		invigorate
supervene	supervention	transcribe	transcript	vine	vintner
surgeon	surgery	transmit	transmission	vinegar	vinaigrette
suspend	suspense	tremble	tremulous	violin	violoncello
suspicion	suspicious	twelve	twelfth	voice	vocal
sustain	sustenance	typhus	typhoid		vociferate
swell	swollen	tyrant	tyranny	weave	weft
syllable	syllabic	unction	unctuous		woven

Lesson 62.		Lesson 64.		Lesson 66.	
sympathy	sympathetic	use	usual	wide	width
synopsis	synoptical	vague	vagary	wise	wizard
syntax	syntactical	vague	vagabond		wisdom
synthesis	synthetical	vale	valley	work	wrought
teach	taught	valour	valorous		wright
tedium	tedious	vain	vanity	wrath	wroth
terminus	terminate	vapour	vaporous	write	wrote
theorem	theoretic	various	variety		writ
thieve	thief	Venice	Venetian		written
tinge	tincture	vertex	vertical		

PART VIII
FIFTEEN SPELLING RULES

PART VIII

FIFTEEN SPELLING RULES

RULE I.—Words ending in a **single accented** consonant double the consonant before an English vowel-suffix: wherever this is necessary in order to preserve the vowel-sound of the accented syllable unaltered.

SHORT FORM OF RULE: Accent on a single final consonant doubles it.

CONSONANT ACCENTED.		VOWEL ACCENTED.	
bar	barring	bear	bearing
bat	batting	bait	baiting
bet	betting	beat	beating
blot	blotted	bloat	bloated
chat	chatting	cheat	cheating
clan	clannish	clown	clownish
clap	clapper	creep	creeper
dim	dimmed	deem	deemed
drum	drummer	dream	dreamer
flit	flitting	float	floating
grin	grinning	groan	groaning
hit	hitting	heat	heating
jar	jarred	jeer	jeered
mad	madden	maid	maiden
mat	matting	meet	meeting
nod	nodded	need	needed
plot	plotting	plait	plaiting
quit	quitting	quoit	quoiting
run	running	rain	raining
sin	sinner	soon	sooner
slop	sloppy	sleep	sleepy
spin	spinner	speak	speaker
stir	stirred	steer	steered
stop	stopper	steep	steeper
swim	swimmer	steam	steamer
wet	wetting	wait	waiting

CONSONANT ACCENTED.		VOWEL ACCENTED.	
abet	abetting	await	awaiting
appal	appalling	appeal	appealing
begin	beginning	bemoan	bemoaning
compel	compelling	conceal	concealing
debar	debarred	demean	demeaned
excel	excelled	exceed	exceeded
forbid	forbidding	forbear	forbearing
instil	instilled	impair	impaired
outwit	outwitting	outpour	outpouring
permit	permitting	pertain	pertaining
refer	referred	repair	repaired
repel	repelled	repeal	repealed
submit	submitting	succeed	succeeding
intermit	intermitted	invalid	invalided

EXCEPTIONS.—**Gas** forms its plural **gases**.
Wool doubles the l in **woollen**, although the sound does not require it.

RULE II.—Words ending in a single consonant but not accented on the last syllable do not double the consonant when added to; because the vowel-sound remains of itself unaltered.

SHORT FORM: Unaccented final consonant is **not** doubled.

alter	altering	alias	aliases
beggar	beggary	benefit	benefited
bigot	bigoted	consider	considering
cater	caterer	develop	developed
chasten	chasteneth	encumber	encumbered
foster	fostering	inherit	inheriting
garden	gardener	interpret	interpreter
limit	limited	minister	ministering
murmur	murmuring	revisit	revisited
quiet	quieter	surrender	surrendered

EXCEPTIONS.—**Worship** makes **worshipped, worshipping, worshipper.**
Bias makes **biassed** and **unbiassed.**

Rule III.—Words ending in a single l double the l before an English vowel-suffix.

apparel	apparelled	jewel	jeweller
barrel	double-barrelled	label	labelled
cancel	cancelling	libel	libeller
chisel	chiselled	marshal	marshalling
dishevel	dishevelled	model	modelled
duel	duelling	quarrel	quarrelling
enamel	enamelled	revel	reveller
equal	equalled	rival	unrivalled
gambol	gambolled	shovel	shovelling
imperil	imperilled	travel	traveller

Exception.—Parallel makes paralleled and unparalleled.

Rule IV.—Words ending in e drop the e before a **vowel-suffix** but retain it before a **consonant-suffix**.

Short Form : Final e is dropped before a **vowel**.

	VOWEL-SUFFIX.	CONSONANT-SUFFIX.		VOWEL-SUFFIX.	CONSONANT-SUFFIX.
abate	abating	abatement	love	lovable	lovely
blame	blamable	blameworthy	move	movable	movement
care	caring	careless	name	naming	nameless
defile	defiling	defilement	praise	praising	praiseworthy
excite	excitable	excitement	starve	starving	starveling
free	free-er	freedom	tame	tam-er	tameless
hate	hating	hateful	value	valuable	valueless

Exceptions.—(i) Words ending in **ce** and **ge** retain the e before the suffixes **able** and **ous** : this being necessary in order to keep the soft sound of c and g.

advantage	advantageous	notice	noticeable
change	changeable	outrage	outrageous
charge	chargeable	peace	peaceable
courage	courageous	pronounce	pronounceable
manage	manageable	trace	traceable
marriage	marriageable	service	serviceable

Singe and **swinge** retain the **e** before **ing**. This is to distinguish their present participles from those of **sing** and **swing**.

| singe | singeing | sing | singing |
| swinge | swingeing | swing | swinging |

(ii) Words ending in **ee**, **oe**, **ye**, retain the final **e** before **ing**.

fee	feeing	guarantee	guaranteeing
flee	fleeing	hoe	hoeing
free	freeing	shoe	shoeing
see	seeing	toe	toeing
agree	agreeing	dye	dyeing
decree	decreeing	eye	eyeing

while **agree** retains it even in **agreeable**.

(iii) Words ending in **ie** change the ending into **y** before **ing**.

| die | dying | tie | tying |
| lie | lying | vie | vying |

(iv) **Glue** makes **gluey**.

(v) Final **e** is dropped before a consonant-suffix in the following words:—

abridge	abridgment	one	only
acknowledge	acknowledgment	paste	pastry
awe	awful	side	sidle
due	duly	true	truly
fore	forward	while	whilst
judge	judgment	whole	whol-ly
lose	lost	wide	width
nine	ninth	wise	wisdom
nose	nostril	woe	woful

RULE V.—Words ending in **y** with a **consonant** before it change the **y** into **i** when a suffix is added; but, if the **y** has a **vowel** before it, **no** change takes place.

SHORT FORM: Consonant + y changes;
Vowel + y does **not** change.

Y WITH A CONSONANT BEFORE IT.		Y WITH A VOWEL BEFORE IT.	
ally	allies	alley	alleys
ally	allied	allay	allayed
bury	burial	betray	betrayal
cheery	cheerily	coy	coyly
cherry	cherries	chimney	chimneys
descry	descried	destroy	destroyed
embody	embodiment	employ	employment
envy	envies	envoy	envoys
fairy	fairies	foray	forays
greedy	greedier	grey	greyer
jelly	jellies	journey	journeys
jolly	jollity	joy	joyful
marry	married	money	moneyed
penny	penniless	pay	payment
pity	pitiful	play	playful
pry	pried	pray	prayed
query	queries	quay	quays
rely	relies	relay	relays
silly	sillier	slay	slayer
try	tries	tray	trays

EXCEPTIONS.—(i) Where the suffix begins with i (as ing, ish, ist), the y is always retained, to prevent two i's from coming together. **Triing** would not look well.

cry	crying	ally	allying
dry	drying	baby	babyish
fry	frying	carry	carrying
ply	plying	copy	copyist
try	trying	envy	envying

(ii) In the following words y is changed into i, although the y has a vowel before it :—

day	daily	say	said
gay	gaiety	say	saith
gay	gaily	slay	slain
lay	laid	stay	staid
pay	paid	array	[ar-]raiment

(iii) In the following words y remains unchanged, although it has a consonant before it :—

dry	dryly	dryness
shy	shyly	shyness
sly	slyly	slyness

RULE VI.—Words ending in ll lose one l when they are compounded. Thus full + fill = fulfil. To this rule, however, there are many exceptions.

SHORT FORM : Double ll loses one l when compounded.

all	almighty	dwell	dwelt	install	instalment
all	almost	fill	fulfil	roll	enrol
all	alone	full	awful	skill	skilful
all	already	full	bagful	smell	smelt
all	also	full	bashful	spell	gospel
all	although	full	careful	spill	spilt
all	altogether	full	fulfil	thrall	enthral
all	always	full	ful-ly	thrall	thraldom
all	withal	full	fulness	till	until
bull	bulrush	full	pocketful	well	welcome
chill	chilblain	full	skilful	well	welfare
chill	chil-ly	full	wilful	will	wilful
dull	dul-ly	full	wonderful		
dull	dulness	hill	hil-ly		

EXCEPTIONS.—In the following compounds ll is retained :—

all	allspice	mill	millrace	stall	forestall
bell	bellman	mill	millstone	still	standstill
call	miscall	mill	treadmill	still	stillborn
call	recall	mill	windmill	still	stillness
fall	befall	roll	unroll	tall	tallness
fall	downfall	sell	undersell	tell	foretell
fall	waterfall	shrill	shrillness	well	farewell
fall	windfall	skull	numskull	well	unwell
hill	downhill	small	smallness	well	wellbeing
hill	uphill	spell	spellbound	will	goodwill
ill	illness	stall	bookstall		

Rule VII.—When the diphthong made up of i and e is sounded so as to rhyme with *key*, it is always written ie; unless it comes after the letter c, in which case it is written ei.

Short Form : When the diphthong rhymes with *key*
The i must go before the e,
Unless the diphthong follows c.

achieve	lief	relief	after c.
belief	liege	relieve	
believe	mien	reprieve	ceiling
brief	mischief	retrieve	conceit
chief	mischievous	shield	conceive
field	niece	siege	deceit
fiend	piece	thief	deceive
fierce	pier	thieve	perceive
grief	pierce	wield	receipt
grieve	priest	yield	receive

Exceptions.—**Either, neither, plebeian, seize, weird.**

Many people say *īther, nīther*. These two words are therefore also given under Rule VIII.

Rule VIII.—When the diphthong has any other sound but that of *key*, the e always goes before the i.

deign	freight	leisure	skein
cider	heifer	neigh	sleight
eight	height	neighbour	surfeit
either	heinous	neither	their
feign	heir	nonpareil	veil
feint	inveigh	reign	vein
forfeit	inveigle	rein	weigh

Rule IX.—The prefixes **dis** and **mis** are never **diss** and **miss**.

That is to say, whenever you find **diss** or **miss**, you know that the second s is not part of the prefix but the first letter of the word to which dis or mis is prefixed.

Short Form : **Dis is dis; and mis is mis.**

dis-arm	dis-satisfied	mis-applied	mis-shapen
dis-band	dis-sect	mis-behave	mis-spell
dis-cern	dis-semble	mis-chance	mis-state
dis-dain	dis-sent	mis-deed	
dis-enchant	dis-similar	mis-fortune	
dis-franchise	dis-sociate	mis-giving	
dis-gorge	dis-solve	mis-hap	
dis-hearten	dis-solute	mis-inform	
dis-inherit	dis-suade	mis-lay	
dis-miss	dis-syllable	mis-represent	

RULE X.—Adjectives ending in **ble** make nouns ending in **bility**.

a-ble becomes a-bility : amia-ble, amia-bility
i-ble becomes i-bility : possi-ble, possi-bility
o-ble becomes o-bility : no-ble, no-bility
u-ble becomes u-bility : volu-ble, volu-bility

This is because **ble** is the English form of the Latin ending **bilis**, which made nouns ending in **bilitas**. Take for example:—

Latin. **No-bilis** makes noun **no-bilitas**
English. **No-ble** makes noun **no-bility**

affable	affability	liable	liability
amiable	amiability	mutable	mutability
applicable	applicability	notable	notability
capable	capability	placable	placability
impenetrable	impenetrability	pliable	pliability
insatiable	insatiability	practicable	practicability
inscrutable	inscrutability	probable	probability
insuperable	insuperability	respectable	respectability
intractable	intractability	sociable	sociability
irritable	irritability	stable	stability

compatible	compatibility	invincible	invincibility
credible	credibility	invisible	invisibility
eligible	eligibility	irascible	irascibility
fallible	fallibility	legible	legibility
feasible	feasibility	plausible	plausibility
flexible	flexibility	possible	possibility
incorrigible	incorrigibility	responsible	responsibility
indestructible	indestructibility	risible	risibility
indivisible	indivisibility	sensible	sensibility
intelligible	intelligibility	susceptible	susceptibility

noble nobility

soluble solubility | voluble volubility

Note.—There are many adjectives in ble that form nouns simply by adding **ness** ; but, as this makes no change in their spelling, they need not be noticed here.

RULE XI.—Adjectives (and some nouns) ending in **ant** and **ent** make nouns ending in **ance** (or **ancy**) and **ence** (or **ency**).

ant becomes **ance**	:	abund-ant, abund-ance
or **ancy**	:	relev-ant, relev-ancy
ent becomes **ence**	:	pres-ent, pres-ence
or **ency**	:	expedi-ent, expedi-ency

The Latin form of **ance** or **ancy** is **antia**.
of **ence** or **ency** is **entia**.

abundant	abundance	brilliant	brilliancy
assistant	assistance	buoyant	buoyancy
defiant	defiance	discrepant	discrepancy
elegant	elegance	expectant	expectancy
exorbitant	exorbitance	flippant	flippancy
extravagant	extravagance	occupant	occupancy
fragrant	fragrance	piquant	piquancy
ignorant	ignorance	relevant	relevancy
important	importance	vacant	vacancy
significant	significance	vagrant	vagrancy
absent	absence	agent	agency
confident	confidence	consistent	consistency
convenient	convenience	constituent	constituency
correspondent	correspondence	decent	decency
different	difference	despondent	despondency
innocent	innocence	frequent	frequency
patient	patience	lenient	leniency
prevalent	prevalence	president	presidency
resident	residence	sufficient	sufficiency
violent	violence	urgent	urgency

Note.—(i) In some cases the same adjective makes two nouns : one in **ce**, the other in **cy**.

relevant	relevance	relevancy
complacent	complacence	complacency
excellent	excellence	excellency
transparent	transparence	transparency

(ii) **Ascendant** ought to be spelled **-ent**; and consequently the noun made from it is **ascendency**. The misspelling **ascendant** arose from confusion with **descendant**.

RULE XII.—Adjectives and some nouns ending in **ate** make nouns ending in **acy**.

ate becomes **acy**; adequ-ate, adequ-acy.

acy generally represents the Latin form of atio.

accurate	accuracy	intricate	intricacy
adequate	adequacy	inveterate	inveteracy
advocate	advocacy	legitimate	legitimacy
celibate	celibacy	magistrate	magistracy
confederate	confederacy	obdurate	obduracy
curate	curacy	obstinate	obstinacy
degenerate	degeneracy	pirate	piracy
delicate	delicacy	prelate	prelacy
effeminate	effeminacy	private	privacy
intimate	intimacy	profligate	profligacy

RULE XIII.—Many words ending in **er** and **or** drop the **e** and the **o** in their derivatives.

The following is a fairly complete list:—

administer	administration	idolater	idolatry
	administrative	integer	integral
	administrator		integrity
anger	angry	leper	leprous
arbiter	arbitrary	master	mistress
	arbitrate	monster	monstrous
baluster	balustrade	neuter	neutral
barometer	barometrical	palter	paltry
brother	brethren	proper	propriety
carpenter	carpentry	register	registrar
cumber	cumbrous		registration
cylinder	cylindrical		registry
diameter	diametrical	remember	remembrance
disaster	disastrous	sequester	sequestrate
dower	dowry	sober	sobriety
enchanter	enchantress	songster	songstress
encumber	encumbrance	sunder	sundry
enter	entrance	thermometer	thermometrical
	entry	tiger	tigress
hinder	hindrance	waiter	waitress
hunter	huntress	winter	wintry
idolater	idolatrous	wonder	wondrous

actor	actress	executor	executrix
ambassador	ambassadress	preceptor	preceptress
ancestor	ancestral	proprietor	proprietress
	ancestry	prosecutor	prosecutrix
doctor	doctrine	testator	testatrix
emperor	empress	traitor	traitress

Note.—It will of course be understood that there are many more words, both in **er** and **or**, which do *not* undergo this change.

RULE XIV.—Some nouns ending in **le** after a consonant have dropped a vowel between the consonant and the **l**. This lost vowel is usually restored in their derivatives.

The most common lost vowel is **u**. Thus, the word **angle** stands for **ang-u-le** (*Lat.* **angulus**); and has for its derivative **angul-ar**.

angle	angular	parable	parabolic
apostle	apostolic	particle	particular
castle	castellated	scruple	scrupulous
circle	circular	spectacle	spectacular
constable	constabulary	strangle	strangulation
epistle	epistolary	table	tabular
fable	fabulous		tabulate
miracle	miraculous	title	titular
muscle	muscular	triangle	triangular
oracle	oracular	vocable	vocabulary

RULE XV.—Adjectives ending in **le** after a consonant make adverbs by adding **y**; the **e** being dropped, according to Rule IV.

All other adjectives make adverbs by adding **ly** (but remember Rule V.)

able	abl-y	legible	legibl-y
ample	ampl-y	noble	nobl-y
audible	audibl-y	passable	passabl-y
contemptible	contemptibl-y	respectable	respectabl-y
credible	credibl-y	simple	simpl-y
double	doubl-y	single	singl-y
favourable	favourabl-y	subtle	subtl-y
forcible	forcibl-y	treble	trebl-y
gentle	gentl-y	triple	tripl-y
idle	idl-y	visible	visibl-y

accidental	accidental-ly	loyal	loyal-ly
cool	cool-ly	natural	natural-ly
cruel	cruel-ly	pale	pale-ly
evasive	evasively	pretty	prettily
evident	evidently	silly	sillily
guilty	guiltily	sole	sole-ly
happy	happily	stale	stale-ly
haughty	haughtily	substantial	substantial-ly
hostile	hostile-ly	vile	vile-ly
humane	humanely	whole	whol-ly

PART IX
SIDE-LIGHTS FROM THE HISTORY OF THE ENGLISH LANGUAGE

PART IX

SIDE-LIGHTS FROM THE HISTORY OF THE ENGLISH LANGUAGE

ITS ELEMENTS AND THE SPELLING OF THEM

1. **Introductory.**—The language which we speak in the British Isles is called **English**. It was brought over to this country in the middle of the fifth century,—more than 1400 years ago. It was brought over from the north-west of Europe,—from the country which lies round the mouths of the Elbe and the Weser, by rude tribes of men who were called **Angles, Saxons,** and **Jutes**. These men were sea-rovers, pirates, warriors; and they came to Great Britain to seize the land and the wealth of its inhabitants. These inhabitants were **Celts**, and spoke a language very different from that spoken by the Angles. The language of the Celts was, in fact, the same as that now spoken by the Welsh in Wales, by the Highlanders in the north and west of Scotland, by the Erse in the west of Ireland, and by the Bretons in Brittany in the west of France.

> On the coast of the Baltic, between the Bay of Kiel and the Little Belt, there is a district called **Angeln** to this day.

2. **The English Language.**—But the language brought over by the Angles is what we now call **English**; and it is quite different from any Celtic language, wherever it is found. The Jutes and Saxons

spoke the same language with very slight differences. **English** settled first of all with the Jutes in Kent; afterwards in other parts of the island. The Angles settled chiefly in the east of England, and were divided into two great tribes called the **North Folk** and the **South Folk**; and these names were gradually shortened into **Norfolk** and **Suffolk**, which are now the names of the two East Anglian counties. The Saxons settled chiefly in the south of Great Britain; and, as they increased and multiplied much more than the Jutes or Angles, they gave their name to much larger parts of the country. Thus the kingdom of the West Saxons came to be known as **Wessex** (and Alfred the Great was the most famous king of Wessex); the kingdom of the South Saxons as **Sussex**; of the Middle Saxons as **Middlesex**; and of the East Saxons as **Essex**.

(i) The Jutes settled chiefly in Kent and the Isle of Wight.

(ii) The word *South* takes many forms. It appears as *Sus* in *Sussex* (=South Saxons); as *Sur* in *Surrey* (=South Rice, or "South Kingdom"); as *Sud* in *Sudbury* (=South Borough); and as *Sod* in *Sodor* (=South Oer, or "South Islands").

3. **Different Kinds of English.**—The English spoken by the Angles differed slightly from the English spoken by the Jutes; and this, again, from that spoken by the Saxons. These differences increased when these tribes settled in parts of the country at great distances from each other; and hence were unable to hold much communication with each other. Each tribe kept itself to itself; and travelling was very difficult, for there were few or no roads in those early times. We must also remember that it would take a man as many weeks to travel from Norwich to Winchester as it would take him hours in the present day. Hence the Angles spoke one kind— or **dialect**—of English; the Jutes another kind; the Saxons another. And, indeed, the dialect of the West Saxons differed greatly from that of the East Saxons. Each of these peoples, moreover, had different ways of pronouncing their own language—and more especially, different ways of pronouncing the vowels.

4. **The Spelling of English.**—The English language was, most probably, not written at all in this island till the eighth century. And, just as there were different ways of pronouncing, so there were also different ways of writing down the words. Thus, in the north of England, a highland region was called a *wold*; in the south, the same word appears in the form of *weald*. One very marked difference between the dialects of the north and the south of England is found in the fact that the north prefers a hard sound to a soft sound. Thus, in the north, people said *scuffle*, but, in the south, *shuffle*; in the north, they said *rig*, *scabby*, and *skirt* for *ridge*, *shabby*, and *shirt*. That is to say, the words *scuffle* and *shuffle*, *rig* and *ridge*, were originally the same words; but, by a difference first in pronunciation, and then in spelling, they came to be looked upon as two different words with different meanings. The same is the case with *kirk* and *church*; *drill* and *thrill*; *mash* and *mess*; *bank* and *bench*; *sprig* and *spray*; *waggon* and *wain*: the first of each of these couples was simply the hard northern way of pronouncing the word.

5. **The Elements of English.**—The English language does not consist entirely of English words. There are many kinds of words in it: Latin, Celtic, Scandinavian, and many other different kinds. The Danish Invasion in the eighth century—it began in 787—brought in a large number of Scandinavian words. The Norman Invasion of 1066 introduced a very large number of Norman-French words. The Revival of Learning—a peaceful kind of invasion, which began in the sixteenth century—introduced an enormous number of Latin words. Last of all, the enterprise, the daring, and the commercial pursuits of our countrymen have for several centuries sent them into every part of the known world; and they have brought from every continent, and almost from every country under the sun, new words to enrich our language. India, Turkey, Persia, Arabia, the two Americas, and many other lands have sent to us their contributions of new words.

6. **Pure English.**—The following words are perfectly pure

English, and have resided in this country for many centuries. The spelling of them is never self-consistent; and therefore every word requires to be looked at by itself, and remembered for itself.

Lesson 1.

ache	astonished	believe	borrow
acknowledge	awry	bequeathe	bough
acorn	banns	bereave	brittle
aghast	barley	beseech	buxom
anvil	befal	bleach	chaffinch
aspen	belie	blithe	chary

(i) **aghast** is connected with *ghost*.
(ii) **awry** = "on the twist." The verb *wry* has as its diminutive *wriggle*.
(iii) **bequeathe** comes from the old verb *quoth*.
(iv) **beseech** comes from *seek*.
(v) **buxom** meant formerly *pliable, obedient*.

Lesson 2.

chilblain	donkey	errand	flight
clothe	dotage	feather	fortnight
cripple	drizzle	ferry	fulfil
daisy	drowsy	feud	gainsay
darling	either	fieldfare	gallows
doff	empty	fiend	garlic

(i) **chilblain** = a blain (or blister) produced by cold.
(ii) **clothe** is the verb from *cloth*; as **wreathe** from *wreath*.
(iii) **daisy** = day's eye.
(iv) **darling** = dear + el + ing; a double diminutive.
(v) **doff** = do + off. So don = do + on; dout = do + out.
(vi) **ferry** = a place across which one is made to *fare*. **Fieldfare** = a bird that *fares* (goes) in the fields.
(vii) **flight** is connected with *fly*; as **sight** is with *see*.
(viii) **garlic** = gar (spear) leek. *Gar* is a form of *gore*.

Lesson 3.

giggle	gossamer	handicraft	height
gnarled	gristle	harrier	heyday
gnaw	haggard	havoc	hiccough
good-bye	haggle	hazel	holiday
gosling	hallow	heavy	honey
gospel	halve	heifer	hundred

(i) **gosling** = goose + el + ing.
(ii) **gospel** = spell (story) of God.
(iii) **harrier** = a dog for *hares*. So **lawyer** from *law*.
(iv) **heavy** from *heave*. So also **heaven**.
(v) **height** from *high*. So **neighbour** from *nigh*.

Lesson 4.

icicle	ladle	minnow	nostril
impound	lodestar	mongrel	nozzle
ingot	lodestone	mould	numb
innings	manifold	nought	orchard
knoll	mermaid	naughty	paddock
knowledge	mildew	nightingale	pebble

(i) **impound** = put in the *pound*.
(ii) **lodestar** = leading star.
(iii) **mermaid** = maid of the *mere* (lake).
(iv) **naughty** = of *naught* (or nought).
(v) **nostril** = nose-drill (hole). **Nozzle** = little nose.

Lesson 5.

periwinkle	rudder	sheriff	stalk
pewter	scullery	shield	steadfast
picnic	scythe	sieve	stirrup
quagmire	seldom	speech	sultry
quail	sheath	spider	swerve
reckon	shepherd	spinster	swivel

(i) **quagmire** = quake-mire.
(ii) **scull** is another form of *swill*. Hence **scullery** = *swillery*.
(iii) **shepherd** = sheep-herd. **Sheriff** = shire-reeve.
(iv) **speech** is connected with *speak*; as **breach** is with *break*.

Lesson 6.

tawdry	tithe	unkempt	Wednesday
thatch	tongue	vixen	weird
thief	trough	walnut	whey
thorough	Tuesday	wassail	willow
threshold	twirl	weapon	winsome
tilth	twitch	weasel	withhold

(i) **tawdry** is a contraction for St. Audrey—a short form of St. Etheldrida, who founded Ely Cathedral.
(ii) **thorough** is another form of *through*.
(iii) **threshold** = thrashwold—the piece of wood which is *thrashed* or beaten by the feet of those who enter the house.
(iv) **tilth** from *till*, to cultivate. Agriculture was called by the Saxons *earth-tilth*.
(v) **tithe**, not from *ten*, but from *ti*, the Danish for *ten*.
(vi) **tongue** was in O.E. written *tong*. The *ue* was a tail given it in imitation of the French *langue*.
(vii) **unkempt** = uncombed.
(viii) **vixen** is the feminine of *fox*.
(ix) **walnut** = foreign nut. The Cymri of the West were called by the Saxons *wealhas* (foreigners); hence the name *Welsh*.
(x) **Wednesday** = the day of Woden or Odin, the Norse god of war. Hence also *Wednesbury*.
(xi) **withhold** = to keep *back*. *With* has also the sense of *back* in *withdraw*.

Lesson 7.

woad	wrist	yearn	yoke
wrench	writhe	yeast	yolk
wrestle	wroth	yeoman	yore
wriggle	wych-elm	yield	yule

(i) **woad** was a plant used as a blue dye-stuff.
(ii) **wrench** is a form of *wring*, which again gives *wrong* (= that which is *wrenched* or *wrung* from the right).
(iii) **wrestle** is the continuative of *wrest*. (The noun is **wrist**.)
(iv) **wroth** = full of *wrath*.
(v) **wych-elm**, a drooping elm. (It has no connection with *witch*.)
(vi) **yolk** comes from *yellow*.
(vii) **yore** (= in old years) comes from *year*.

THE ENGLISH LANGUAGE 113

7. Low German Words.—Our language has also received a few words from that part of Germany which is called **Low Germany**. This part consists of the low plains which lie around the Baltic Sea; and the German spoken here is called **Low German**. The following are some of these Low-German words.

Lesson 8.

bounce	hawker	rabbit	slight
bully	massacre	rabble	sprout
bumble-bee	muddle	scold	supper
flounder	pamper	shudder	tallow
groat	peer	slender	wafer

(i) **groat** (=a large penny) is a form of *great*.
(ii) **hawker** (one who sells) is a form of *huckster*.
(iii) **massacre**, though a Low-German word, has had its spelling influenced by French.
(iv) **peer**=to *pry* into. Peer (a nobleman) comes from Lat. *par* (equal), through French.

8. Dutch Words.—We have also borrowed words from the Dutch; and several of these relate to the sea and sea-faring. The following are a few.

Lesson 9.

ballast	doit	holster	morass
beleaguer	drugget	hustle	stiver
blunderbuss	easel	isinglass	trigger
bumpkin	firkin	jerkin	wainscot
cracknel	hoarding	landscape	yacht

(i) **blunderbuss** is an odd misspelling of *donderbus* (=thunder-box).
(ii) **bumpkin** is the diminutive of *boom*. Hence it means a wooden-headed fellow.
(iii) **doit** is a small Dutch coin. (Perhaps a form of *dot*.)
(iv) **easel** (a support for pictures) is a diminutive of *ass*.
(v) **morass** is a word connected with *moor*.

I

9. Scandinavian Words.—Our language has received a very large number of words from Norway and Denmark. The first invasion of the Danes and their words took place in 787; and, from that time, they settled in larger and larger numbers on the east coasts of England and Scotland. Hence it happens that there are hundreds of places in the east of England whose names end in **by**, which is the Danish for "town." Such are **Selby, Appleby, Whitby, Grimsby,** and many more. Danish kings sat on the throne of England from 1015 to 1042; and, in the Danelagh, there was more Danish blood than English. The following are some of these Danish words.

Lesson 10.

askew	dazzle	gaunt	harbour
blemish	eider-duck	geyser	hawser
bloater	flippant	glimpse	hustings
bulwark	forage	gnash	jersey
clumsy	furlough	grimace	kidney
dastard	garish	grovel	larboard

(i) **bulwark** = bole-work, a work made by the *boles* or stumps of trees.
(ii) **dastard** comes from the verb *daze*, the frequentative of which is dazzle.
(iii) **furlough** = leave given to a soldier. It is connected with *leave*.
(iv) **geyser** = gusher.
(v) **glimpse** is a form of *glimmer*.
(vi) **grimace** is connected with *grin*.
(vii) **hustings** = house-thing (a parliament or council in a house).
(viii) **larboard** means the *left* side of the ship, looking from the stern.

Lesson 11.

luncheon	scream	squabble	tight
mawkish	screech	squander	wail
niggard	shriek	squeak	walrus
paltry	skewer	squeal	wherry
quandary	sleight	thrift	windlass
rinse	sneer	tidings	wraith

(i) **quandary** (perplexity) is connected with *wander*.
(ii) **rinse** = cleanse.

(iii) **scream, screech,** and **shriek** are all fundamentally the same word.
(iv) **sleight** (from *sleigh* or *sly*) = slyness.
(v) **sneer** has, as its frequentative, *snarl*.
(vi) **squeak** is allied to *quack*.
(vii) **thrift** comes from *thrive*; as **theft** from *thieve*.
(viii) **wail** is connected with *wo!*
(ix) **walrus** = whale-horse.

10. German Words.—Our language has adopted very few pure German words; but it contains a good number of words which came originally from Germany, but which seem to have resided for some time in France, and to have thus put on a French look, or clothed themselves in a French spelling. The following words are of both kinds.

LESSON 12.

PURE GERMAN.	GERMAN IN A FRENCH DRESS.		
camellia	allegiance	banquet	chamberlain
fuchsia	ambassador	bivouac	chamois
meerschaum	bagatelle	bouquet	coterie
waltz	balloon	burgess	enamel
zinc	ballot	carousal	equerry

(i) **meerschaum** (sea-foam) is the name given to a fine clay, found in Greece, out of which pipes are made.
(ii) **ambassador** has been influenced in its spelling both by French and Spanish.
(iii) **balloon** is a big ball; **ballot** a little ball.
(iv) **banquet** comes from *bank* (bench), through Fr. *banc*.
(v) **equerry** has nothing to do with the Lat. *equus*, a horse; it comes from an Old German word *scura*, a shed or cover.

LESSON 13.

eschew	freight	liege	patrol
etiquette	gaiter	marchioness	scabbard
fief	guarantee	marquis	sturgeon
filbert	harangue	minion	treachery
franchise	harbinger	motley	warrant

(i) **eschew** is another form of *shy*.
(ii) **etiquette** is only a Frenchified way of writing *ticket*, which is connected with the verb *stick*.
(iii) **fief** means land held of a superior lord.
(iv) **franchise** = freedom, originally the freedom and rights of the Franks, an old Germanic tribe.
(v) **guarantee** is another form of **warrant**.
(vi) **harbinger**, a person sent on to get lodgings. The word is connected with *harbour*, which once meant an inn. An inn in which provisions could not be obtained was called "Cold Harbour"; and there are many places in England with this name.
(vii) **marquis** is a nobleman who guards the *marches* or boundaries of a country. Another spelling is **marquess**.
(viii) **sturgeon** is a word connected with *stir*. It is so called from "stirring up the mud."

11. **Celtic Words.**—There is in our language a considerable number of Celtic words—that is, of words which form part of the language of the Early Britons, who inhabited this island long before the Angles, Saxons, and Jutes came. The names of our rivers, lakes, and mountains are generally Celtic. But, in addition to the Celtic words given to our language by the Britons, a number have come from Ireland, and a few from Scotland. These last have found their way into English chiefly through Sir Walter Scott's works. A few have also come to us from France; and these have accordingly a French spelling.

Lesson 14.

barracks	capercailzie	flannel	penguin
barrier	caricature	gillie	pibroch
bauble	chariot	javelin	pilchard
billiards	coracle	knuckle	pottage
bludgeon	dudgeon	mackintosh	ptarmigan
boisterous	earnest	maggot	skein

(i) **barracks, barrier, billiards, chariot, javelin,** and **pottage** are all Celtic words that have come to us through French.
(ii) **bludgeon** is said to have come from *block*.
(iii) **capercailzie** (a large game bird) means "horse of the wood."
(iv) **caricature** is a Celtic word which has come to us through Italian.

(v) **coracle** = a light round wicker boat.
(vi) **earnest**—this is not the adjective, but the noun with the meaning of *earnest-penny* or *pledge*.
(vii) **gillie**, a page or attendant.
(viii) **penguin** (a sea-bird) = "white head." *Pen* in Wales, and *Ben* in Scotland are the Celtic for mountain.
(ix) **pibroch** means a tune played on the bagpipes.

12. **Norman-French Words.**—The Normans invaded this island in 1066, subdued the English, and introduced into this island not only their laws, institutions, and customs, but also their language. Hence several thousands of Norman-French words made their way into our English speech. The Norman-Frenchman tried to learn a little English, and the Englishman tried to learn some Norman-French words and phrases; and thus the two languages became mixed at market, at fairs, and in the churches. In time the two languages got to run in couples—the one word going with the other to explain it; and we had such phrases as **aid and abet, will and testament, wright and carpenter.** This double phrasing is very evident in our Prayer-book, where we have such couples as **acknowledge and confess, dissemble nor cloak, humble and lowly,** where one of the words is French, and the other is English. The French words introduced by the Normans gradually made themselves at home in our language; and they are now hardly to be distinguished from ordinary English words, though many of them have a French spelling. (It must not be forgotten that French itself is a kind of Latin—very much altered, especially in the endings.)

LESSON 15.

abeyance	affinity	allege	arraign
abridge	affluence	announce	artillery
achieve	aggressive	annual	assailant
address	aggrieve	appease	assuage
adieu	agreeable	apprentice	atrocity
adroit	alien	aquiline	attorney

(i) **adieu** = I commend you à Dieu (= to God).
(ii) **aquiline** is from Lat. *aquila*, an eagle.

Lesson 16.

artillery	beverage	campaign	chateau
avalanche	biscuit	carnage	chevalier
avaricious	bugle	carrion	chief
average	bureau	ceremony	chivalry
beauty	burglar	challenge	circuit
benefice	caitiff	chancellor	colleague

(i) **avalanche**, a mass of snow which goes down *ad vallem* (= to the valley).
(ii) **biscuit**, from Lat. *bis coctus* (= twice baked).
(iii) **bugle** meant originally *an ox's horn*.
(iv) **burglar** comes from Fr. *bourg*, a town.
(v) **chief**, from Lat. *caput*, through Fr. *chef*.

Lesson 17.

condescend	crevice	despair	disparage
conduit	curfew	despatch	dissimilar
conscience	dandelion	detriment	dissuade
counterfeit	deceive	discern	docile
courage	deity	disciple	dowager
courier	delicious	dishevelled	dungeon

(i) **courage**, from Lat. *cor*, the heart.
(ii) **courier**, from Lat. *curro*, I run.
(iii) **curfew** = couvre-feu (cover-fire).
(iv) **dandelion** = dent de lion (lion's tooth).
(v) **docile**, from Lat. *doc-eo*, I teach.

Lesson 18.

edify	endeavour	environs	faggot
efficient	enemy	equivalent	fallacy
effrontery	engine	esquire	fealty
emolument	ennoble	exceed	federal
emperor	enterprise	excrescence	feminine
empress	entrails	facetious	fierce

(i) **esquire** comes from Lat. *scutiger* (= shield-bearer to a knight).
(ii) **fealty** is a Norman-French form of the word *fidelity* (Lat. *fidelitas*). In the same way, the Normans had **leal** for *loyal*; and **real** (in **realm**) for *royal*.

Lesson 19.

flageolet	fugitive	grandeur	ignominy
flunkey	gaol	gratuity	imbecile
foliage	generosity	grieve	immediate
forfeit	Gentile	guttural	immemorial
fragile	glacier	hearse	inaccessible
frontispiece	gorgeous	heritage	incident

(i) **flunkey** originally meant a defender on the *flank*.
(ii) **gaol** (not to be confused with **goal**, a winning-post) comes from the Lat. *gabiola*, a cage.
(iii) **guttural**, from Lat. *guttur*, the throat.

Lesson 20.

incommode	innocent	irreparable	jewel
incredible	innumerable	irrepressible	joust
indissoluble	inseparable	irretrievable	judicious
ineligible	insuperable	issue	kerchief
infallible	inutility	jaundice	languor
inimitable	invincible	jeopardy	lassitude

(i) **innocent** = not hurtful, from Lat. *in* (not) and *noc-ens* (hurtful).
(ii) **inseparable** is connected with *separate*; **insuperable** with *super* (above).
(iii) **jaundice**, from Fr. *jaune*, yellow.
(iv) **jeopardy**—note the eo.

Lesson 21.

laurel	leveret	mackerel	medicine
leal	library	magnanimity	menagerie
legend	lieutenant	maintenance	mercenary
legible	literature	malady	meridian
leisure	litigious	maritime	messenger
lettuce	luminary	matrimony	mineral

(i) **leal** is the Norman-French form of *loyal*.
(ii) **lettuce** (= the milky plant) comes from Lat. *lac*, milk.
(iii) **leveret** (a young hare), from Lat. *lepus*, a hare.
(iv) **litigious** = fond of lawsuits (Lat. *litis*, a lawsuit).
(v) **maintenance** alters the *tain* in *maintain* into *ten*. (Compare **pertain, pertinent.**)
(vi) **mineral** = what is dug out of a *mine*.

Lesson 22.

miscreant	necessary	obey	origin
moiety	negligence	obeisance	pacific
morsel	niece	oblique	palace
municipal	novice	omelet	palfrey
mutiny	nuisance	omnipotent	palpable
mystery	nutritive	onion	paraffine

(i) **moiety** (= a half), from Lat. *medius*, through Fr.
(ii) **morsel**, from Lat. *mordeo*, I bite. Compare *bite, bit.*
(iii) **obey**, from Lat. *obedio*, I listen to. **Obeisance** is the act of reverence (or obedience).
(iv) **onion** is another form of *union*, the name given to a large pearl, because it was the only *one* (Lat. *unus*) of its kind. An onion is shaped like a pearl.

Lesson 23.

parcel	pencil	petition	pontiff
parricide	penury	pigeon	porringer
participle	perceive	pinnacle	portray
peasant	pernicious	pomegranate	portrait
pecuniary	pertain	pommel	prairie
penance	pertinent	poniard	precede

(i) **parcel** comes from Lat. *pars*, a part. Compare *particle*.
(ii) **parricide** (for *patricide*), from Lat. *pater* (a father) and *cida* (a slayer).
(iii) **pertain** makes **pertinent**; as **maintain** makes **maintenance**.
(iv) **pomegranate**, from Lat. *pomum* (an apple) and *granātum* (filled with grains or seeds).
(v) **pommel**, diminutive from Lat. *pomum*, an apple.
(vi) **pontiff** (= the Pope), originally a bridge-maker (Lat. *pons*, a bridge, and *facio*, I make).
(vii) **precede** must be distinguished from *proceed*.

Lesson 24.

precipice	prestige	promenade	pursue
precise	primitive	prominent	purvey
preference	privilege	promise	putrefy
prejudice	prodigal	prorogue	putrid
preliminary	professor	puerile	quarantine
presentiment	proffer	puissant	quatrain

(i) observe the one f in **professor**; the two in **proffer**.

(ii) **prominent** (standing forth), **eminent** (standing out), **imminent** (standing over), all have min.

(iii) **pursue** and **purvey** have the pur (Fr. *pour*) = for.

(iv) **purvey** is another form of *provide*.

(v) **putrefy** has an e; **putrid**, an i.

(vi) **quarantine** is a staying apart for *forty* days (Fr. *quarante*).

(vii) **quatrain** is a stanza of *four* lines (Fr. *quatre*).

Lesson 25.

radical	redoubtable	reprieve	reveal
raisin	refuge	residue	revel
rancour	regicide	resign	reverie
receive	relieve	restaurant	roistering
recommend	reminiscence	reticule	rubric
recruit	repartee	retrieve	russet

(i) **radical** comes from Lat. *radix* (a root), which also gives *radish* and *race*.

(ii) **rancour** keeps the our which it got from French; but the adjective is *rancorous* (with a **cor**).

(iii) **redoubtable** = terrible; from Fr. *redouter* (to fear), which, however, has not the **b**.

(iv) **resign**, like **sign**, **assign**, **consign**, keeps the **gn**.

(v) **reticule**, from Lat. *reticulum*, a little net.

(vi) **reveal** makes *revealing* (with one *l*); **revel** makes *revelling*, with two.

(vii) **reverie**, from Fr. *rêver*, to dream.

(viii) **roister** is connected with *rustic*.

(ix) **rubric**, from Lat. *ruber*, red. The directions in the Book of Common Prayer were called **rubrics**, because they were printed in *red* letters. (Compare *ruby*.)

(x) **russet** is connected with *ruddy*.

Lesson 26.

sacrifice	scutcheon	sergeant	souse
sacrilege	secretary	siege	souvenir
salary	sediment	similar	sovereign
satellite	senate	sluice	stanch
sausage	sepulchre	solicit	stupefy
scissors	sequel	solitary	stupid

(i) **sacrilege** is a profanation of what is *sacred*.

(ii) **salary**, from Lat. *sal*. Hence the phrase "not worth his salt." Sausage and sauce come from the same root, by the change of l into u.

(iii) **scissors**, from Lat. *scindo* (I cut), which also gives *rescind*, etc.

(iv) **scutcheon**, a painted shield, from Lat. *scutum* (a shield). It is also spelled **escutcheon**.

(v) **senate** is an assembly of *senes* (Lat. for *old men*). The same root is found in *senior*, *senator*, etc.

(vi) **sergeant** (from Lat. *servio*, I serve) is a man who serves in the army; **serjeant** (with j), a lawyer who serves at the Bar.

(vii) **sluice**, from Lat. *exclusa*, a flood-gate, to *shut off* water. Connected with it are *exclude*, *exclusion*; but these have not ui.

(viii) **stanch** = to stop (or make *stagnant*) the flow of blood; **staunch** (an *adj.*, with u) = steady, faithful.

(ix) **stupefy** has e; **stupid**, i. Compare **putrefy** and **putrid**.

Lesson 27.

subtle	superstitious	taunt	tissue
succeed	supplement	temptation	tortoise
succulent	suppliant	tenacity	tortuous
suffrage	surfeit	tendril	tourney
suicide	surrender	tenement	tournament
supersede	tabernacle	territory	trammel

(i) **succeed** and **proceed** have eed. **Recede** and **precede** have ede.

(ii) **suicide** = a slayer of self. Lat. *cida* (a slayer), *sui* (of one's self).

(iii) **supersede** comes from Lat. *sedeo*, I sit. **Precede** comes from *cedo*, I go.

(iv) **supplement** has an e; like **tenement**.

(v) **tabernacle**, a diminutive from Lat. *taberna*, a shed.

(vi) **tissue** was cloth interwoven with gold or silver.

(vii) **tortoise** (from Lat. *tortus*, twisted) is so called from its crooked or twisted feet. The same root gives **torture** and **tortuous.**
(viii) **tourney** has **ey** ; **tournament** has an **a.**
(ix) **trammel** makes **trammelled** with two ll's.

Lesson 28.

treason	trousseau	urbanity	vague
trefoil	truculent	usury	valiant
trespass	turbulent	utensil	valour
trestle	tureen	utility	variety
tricolor	unique	vacillation	vegetable
trivial	unison	vagabond	velocity

(i) **trefoil,** a three-leaved plant, like clover. From Lat. *tres* (three) and *folium* (a leaf).
(ii) **trespass,** to pass *beyond* bounds. *Tres* is the French form of the Lat. *trans*, beyond.
(iii) **tricolor** is the national flag of France, with the three colours, red, white, and blue. The Lat. prefix *tri* (=three) is also found in *trident, triangle, triennial, trine,* etc.
(iv) **trivial**=that which belongs to a *trivia* (a place where *three* roads meet). Such a spot was likely to become a meeting-place for gossips.
(v) **trousseau**=a little *truss* or bundle. It has a larger meaning now.
(vi) **urbanity**=such a manner as is found in an *urbs* (Lat. for *city*).
(vii) **usury,** money paid for the use of money.
(viii) **utensil,** from Lat. *utor*, I use. So also **utilise, utility,** etc.
(ix) **vagabond,** from Lat. *vagor*, I wander. From the same root comes **vague.**

Lesson 29.

venerable	vestige	violent	vivify
vengeance	victuals	virulent	vociferation
verify	view	visage	volition
vermilion	vignette	viscount	volley
versify	villain	vitriol	voluntary
vessel	vinegar	vivacity	voyage

(i) **vermilion,** red lead.
(ii) **victuals,** from Lat. *victus*, food ; from *vivo*, I live.
(iii) **vignette** is a small engraving with ornamental borders. From Fr. *vigne*, a vine ; as vine-leaves were freely used in such ornaments.

(iv) **villain**, from Lat. *villanus*, a servant on a *villa* (=farm). From the same root come *villainy* and *village*.
(v) **vinegar** (with an e), from Fr. *vin* (wine) and *aigu* (sharp).
(vi) **virulent** (with a u), from Lat. *virus*, poison.
(vii) **viscount**=a person in *place* of a count or earl. From Lat. *vice*, in place of; and *comes*, a companion (to the heir to the throne).
(viii) **vivify** (with i) must be contrasted with **stupefy** (with e). So **versify** and **putrefy**.
(ix) **volition**, an act of the will; from Lat. *volo*, I will. From the same root comes **voluntary**.

13. **Romance Words.**—There is a large number of words which we have adopted into English from the "Roman" (or Latin) languages spoken in the south of Europe. These languages are called **Romance Languages** by learned men, because they are all direct descendants—with very little change in the family likeness—from Latin, the language spoken by the Romans. (A *romance* itself originally meant simply something written in the *Roman* language—that is, in the kind of *spoken Latin* that was used by the Romans and their neighbours.) Some of these Roman words have come to us through French; some through Italian; and some through Spanish. It is very difficult to trace where they come from; and those given in the following three lists are of doubtful origin.

LESSON 30.

abash	brigade	calibre	entrench
arras	brigand	champagne	frieze
battledoor	brusque	charade	frippery
bayonet	burlesque	chiffonier	gallon
bijou	buttress	embrasure	gibbet
blouse	cabbage	embroider	gingham

(i) **arras**, tapestry hangings made at Arras, in the north of France. Hamlet (IV. i. 9) stabs Polonius through the arras, behind which he is hiding.
(ii) **battledoor**, a corruption of the South French *batador*, a washing-bat or "beetle" for clothes.
(iii) **bayonet**, from the town of Bayonne, in the south of France.

(iv) **bijou**, a jewel or trinket.
(v) **blouse**, a kind of smock-frock.
(vi) **brusque**, rough and sudden in manner.
(vii) **cabbage**, to steal. (Literally, to put into a *cabas*, or basket.)
(viii) **champagne**, the wine made in the province of Champagne, which was so called from its wide plains (Lat. *campus*, a plain).
(ix) **chiffonier**, a cupboard—a place to put rags (*chiffons*) in.
(x) **gingham**, a kind of cotton cloth, originally made at Guingamp, in Brittany (in the west of France).

Lesson 31.

gazette	guzzle	lozenge	ninny
gormandise	harass	magnolia	pedigree
graze	haricot	mantua (It.)	pillory
grouse	harlequin	milliner	pinch
guillotine	jacket	martinet	pistol

(i) **gazette**, an Italian word (meaning originally *a small coin*) which came to us through French.
(ii) **gormandise**, to eat like a glutton.
(iii) **graze**, in the sense of "scraping lightly."
(iv) **guillotine**, the instrument for beheading, called after Dr. Guillotin, the inventor.
(v) **magnolia**, a kind of large laurel, with beautiful flowers and leaves, called after P. Magnol, a French professor of botany.
(vi) **mantua**, a cloak, called after the town of Mantua, in Italy.
(vii) **martinet**, a strict disciplinarian. So called after a strict French officer of the time of Louis XIV.

Lesson 32.

pirouette	roan	savoy (It.)	trice (Sp.)
pittance	rodomontade	scupper	trill
poplin	rusk (Sp.)	sedan-chair	valise
rebuff	sarsaparilla (Sp.)	toper	yam (Port.)
regatta (It.)			

(i) **pirouette**, a quick turn in dancing.
(ii) **pittance**, a small allowance (connected with *petty*).
(iii) **regatta**, a rowing or sailing match.
(iv) **roan**, a kind of red (mostly applied to horses).

(v) **rodomontade**, vain boasting.
(vi) **rusk**, a kind of light bread.
(vii) **savoy**, a kind of cabbage, first brought from Savoy, in the north of Italy.
(viii) **scupper**, a hole through which water runs off the deck of a ship.
(ix) **sedan-chair**, a shut-in chair, carried on poles by two men. Called after the town of Sedan, in the north of France.
(x) **trice**, an instant.
(xi) **valise**, a travelling-bag.
(xii) **yam**, an edible root found in Africa and the West Indies.

14. Latin Words (i).—In the sixteenth and seventeenth centuries, Latin words came into our language in very large numbers— they came in by thousands. A remarkable fact about these Latin words is that they are all rightly and regularly spelt; and that the Latin element in English possesses by far the best spelling. Every sound has its own letter; and each letter has only one sound. It is accordingly not easy to misspell a Latin word. This arises from two circumstances : (*a*) that the Latin language is itself regularly spelt— and possesses a true "orthography";[1] and (*b*) that the Latin words we have borrowed were copied out of books, and were transferred into our language by the help of the EYE, which is the most accurate of all the senses. They were not given by the mouth to the ear; in which case we can never be sure that the mouth pronounces accurately, or that the ear catches correctly what the mouth said. The Latin words we have were mostly copied from books into books; and it was not till they had appeared in books that they passed into the mouths of the people. Hence they were correctly written, and are still correctly spelt. It is, accordingly, almost unnecessary to learn the spelling of Latin words—of which the sound and the symbol are

---

[1] From Gr. *orthos* (right) and *graphē* (a writing). The English part of our language cannot be said to possess an *orthography*, because, in old times, every Saxon scribe wrote pretty much as he pleased, and—to-day—our vowel-sounds are written down in many different ways.

always, or almost always, in accord. A few are given here, merely as specimens.

Lesson 33.

accelerate	apprehend	barrister	circumstance
accommodate	arrogate	belligerent	coincide
adequate	assimilate	calculate	commodious
allude	associate	candidate	compel
anticipate	auxiliary	celebrate	competitor
apparatus	aviary	circumference	connect

(i) **calculate**, from Lat. *calculus*, a pebble. All counting for Roman bankers was done by slaves with bags of pebbles.

(ii) **candidate**, from Lat. *candidus*, white. Competitors for an office wore a white robe when engaged in canvassing.

Lesson 34.

repel	sagacious	subsequent	textile
repudiate	seminary	subterranean	trilateral
retaliate	simile	tacit	unanimous
ridiculous	simulate	terrestrial	vaccinate
rivulet	simultaneous	terrific	veteran
sacrament	soliloquy	testimony	veterinary

(i) **repel** makes *repelling*, with two *ll*'s; **repeal** makes *repealing*, with one.

(ii) **seminary**, a place where *semina* (seeds of learning) are sown.

(iii) **simile** is the Latin word itself for *like*.

15. **Latin Words (ii).**—It will be seen from these few instances, selected from many thousands, that there is no difficulty in learning to spell Latin words. The only apparent difficulty is when to use **double consonants**. The Latin scholar finds no difficulty in this; but the English scholar is obliged to observe the word apart from others, or to make himself acquainted with the spelling and the value of Latin prefixes.

LATIN PREFIXES.

Lesson 35.

Ad (= to) becomes, when united with other words, **ac, af, ag,**

al, an, ap, ar, as, or **at,** according to the nature of initial consonant of the word to which it is joined.

accept	afflict	appeal	assail
accord	aggression	applaud	assign
accommodate	aggravate	apprehend	assist
accomplish	allude	arrive	attain
accumulate	annex	assimilate	attend
address	annul	assume	attract

(i) **accord** = to bring hearts together. *Cor*, the heart.
(ii) **accumulate,** from *ad,* to, and *cumulus,* a heap.
(iii) **afflict,** from *ad,* and *fligo,* I strike.
(iv) **annul,** from *ad,* and *nullus,* none.
(v) **applaud,** from *ad,* and *plaudo,* I clap my hands.
(vi) **arrive,** from *ad ripam* = to the bank.
(vii) **assist** = *sisto ad,* I stand beside.

Lesson 36.

Cum (= with *or* together) becomes **com, con, col, cor,** according to the nature of the consonant it stands before. Before **b, f, m,** or **p,** the form is **com.** It is also found as **co.**

commend	concourse	colleague	coagulate
commerce	conduit	collect	coalesce
compel	confluence	collocate	coexist
compound	congregation	correct	coequal
composite	connect	corrode	cohere
comprehend	consent	corrupt	coincide

(i) **commerce,** from *cum,* with, and *merx,* goods *or* wares.
(ii) **concourse,** a running together. *Cursus,* a running.
(iii) **conduit,** a pipe to *lead* along. From *duco,* I lead. The c in *duco* has been refined into i in its passage through the French language.
(iv) **confluence,** a flowing together. *Fluo,* I flow.
(v) **congregation,** from *grex* (= *greg-s*) a flock.

Lesson 37.

In (= in, on, *or* into) becomes **il, im,** or **ir.** In passing through the French language, it becomes **em** or **en.** (There is also a Latin prefix in which means *not*, as in *inapt* = not apt, *incessant* = not ceasing, etc.).

incur	immigrant	irradiate	engrave
infer	impel	irrigate	enjoin
invade	import	irritate	enjoy
induce	impose	embellish	enkindle
illumine	impress	embrace	enlighten
illusion	improve	embroil	enliven

(i) **incur** = to run on. *Curro*, I run. ("I incur a fine").
(ii) **illumine**, to throw (*lumen*) light on.
(iii) **immigrant**, a person who *migrates* into. An **emigrant** is a person who migrates **e** = out of.
(iv) **import**, I carry into. *Porto*, I carry.
(v) **irradiate**, to throw a *radius* (a ray or rays) on.
(vi) **embellish**, to make *bellus* = beautiful.
(vii) The last three words in the last column are pure English words with a Latin-French prefix.

LESSON 38.

Sub (= under) becomes **suc, suf, sug, sum, sup, sur,** or **sus**.

subject	succumb	summon	suppose
sublet	suffer	supplant	suppress
submerge	suffix	supplement	suspect
succeed	suffuse	supplicate	suspend
succour	suggest	support	sustain

(i) **submerge**, I plunge *under* water. *Mergo*, I plunge.
(ii) **succour** (through French), I *run under* as a support. *Curro*, I run.
(iii) **succumb**, I lie under. *Cumbo*, I lie.
(iv) **suffix**, that which is *fixed under*, or at the end of a word.
(v) **support**, I carry under. *Porto*, I carry.

16. **Italian Words.**—We have borrowed from the Italians a few words. Some of these have come to us direct from the Italian— a few along with the things themselves; others have come to us indirectly, by way of France, and hence have something of a French look. It must not be forgotten that Italian is a direct descendant of Latin—that, in fact, it is a kind of modern Latin. The following are the most important.

K

Lesson 39.

askance	carnival	citadel	dilettanté
auburn	cavalcade	colonnade	fugue
battalion	cavalier	corridor	granite
broccoli	cavalry	cuirass	incarnadine
bulletin	cicerone	ditto	incognito

(i) **broccoli**, the plural of *broccŏlo*, a sprout.

(ii) **cavalcade**, from a Low Latin word, *caballus*, a pack-horse. **Cavalier** and **cavalry** come from the same root.

(iii) **cicerone**, a guide who shows people round. From Cicero, the great Roman orator.

(iv) **ditto**, from Lat. *dictus*, said.

(v) **dilettanté**, a lover of the fine arts. From Lat. *delector*, I take delight in.

(vi) **granite**, from Ital. *granito*, grained or speckled.

(vii) **incarnadine**, to dye red (or *carnation*).

Lesson 40.

influenza	motto	postillion	stiletto
isolate	palette	seraglio	terrace
malaria	parapet	somersault	umbrella
miniature	pianoforte	spinach	vermicelli
mizzen	porcelain	squadron	vidette

(i) **influenza** is simply Italian for *influence*. It was afterwards specially applied to an infectious cold.

(ii) **isolate**, from It. *isola*; from Lat. *insula*, an island. Thus **isolate** and **insulate** are doublets.

(iii) **malaria** = bad air. It is chiefly applied to the pestilential air over the Campagna, a wide stretch of land south of Rome.

(iv) **pianoforte** = *even* (or smooth) and *strong*. From the directions given in music.

(v) **squadron**, from It. *squadra*, square. A short form is **squad**.

(vi) **stiletto** = a little *stilus* or dagger.

(vii) **umbrella**, a diminutive from It. *ombra*; from Lat. *umbra*, a shade. Both name and thing were introduced into London only in the last century. It was at first used merely as a *sun*-shade.

(viii) **vermicelli**, the plural of It. *vermicello*, a little worm.

(ix) **vidette**, a cavalry sentinel. The word has come to us through French, and has hence a French spelling.

17. Spanish and Portuguese Words.—Both the Spanish and Portuguese languages are, like Italian, direct descendants from Latin; and all three languages have a strong family likeness. We have adopted a small number of words from both of these tongues; and a few of them, having come to us by way of France, have put on a French look.

Lesson 41.

alligator	commodore	disembogue	fetish
armada	comrade	domino	flamingo
binnacle	cork	don	flotilla
booby	corvette	doubloon	grandee
capsize	creole	dulcimer	grenade

(i) **alligator** = the lizard. From Sp. *el layarto*; from Lat. *lacertus*, a lizard.
(ii) **booby**, from Sp. *bobo*, a blockhead.
(iii) **commodore**, a Spanish form of the word *commander*. It is now used of the naval rank next to an admiral.
(iv) **comrade**, a chamber-mate, from Lat. *camĕra*, a chamber.
(v) **creole**, a person born in the West Indies, but of European blood.
(vi) **disembogue**, to discharge at the mouth (said of a river). From Sp. *boca*, Lat. *bucca*, the cheek or mouth.
(vii) **domino**, the Spanish for *master*. It is shortened into *Don* (= Mr.). The Portuguese say *Dom*.
(viii) **fetish** = artificial. A Portuguese name for the wooden idols made in West Africa. It is the same word as our *factitious*.
(ix) **flamingo** = the flame-bird. From Sp. *flama*, Lat. *flamma*, a flame.
(x) **grenade** = a small bomb-shell filled with shot (or "grains").

Lesson 42.

lasso	mosquito	port	sherry
matador	negro	punctilio	spaniel
merino	parade	quadrille	tornado
moidore	paragon	quadroon	ultramarine
molasses	parasol	renegade	vanilla

(i) **lasso**, a rope with a noose.
(ii) **matador** = the slayer. It is the name of the man who gives the finishing stroke to the bull in bull-fights. Lat. *macto*, I slay.
(iii) **mosquito**, a little gnat—a diminutive of Sp. *mosca*, a fly.

(iv) **parasol**, from Port. *parar* (to parry) and *sol* (the sun).
(v) **port**, an abbreviation of **O Porto** (=*the* Port), the place from which the wine is shipped.
(vi) **punctilio**=a little point (in behaviour). Sp. *punto*, a point.
(vii) **quadrille**, a dance of four persons. From Lat. *quatuor*, four; through Spanish. The same prefix is found in **quadrangle, quadrant, quadroon** (a person with a fourth part of coloured blood), **quadruped**, etc.
(viii) **sherry** = the wine of Xeres (a port near Cadiz), where it is shipped.
(ix) **spaniel** = a Spanish dog.
(x) **tornado** = a revolving hurricane. From Sp. *tornar*, to turn.
(xi) **ultramarine**, sky-blue, literally "beyond the sea." Lat. *ultra* (beyond) and *maré* (the sea).

18. **Greek Words.**—Our language has adopted from Greek a considerable number of words—most of them relating to some part of the different sciences. Many of them are in common use; and it is important that we should make ourselves acquainted with the spelling of them. They are, in general, of a correct and regular spelling, and present very little difficulty. The following are some of the most usual.

Lesson 43.

acrobat	anachronism	antagonist	archaic
æsthetic	analyse	antipathy	archipelago
allopathy	anarchy	antipodes	aristocracy
alphabet	anecdote	antithesis	arithmetic
amphibious	anemoné	apology	arsenic
amphitheatre	anonymous	archæology	asphalt

(i) **acrobat** means "one who walks on tip-toe."
(ii) **allopathy** is opposed to **homœopathy**. The first is a treatment "by unlikes"; the second "by likes."
(iii) **alphabet**. The first two letters in Greek are *alpha, beta*.
(iv) **amphibious**, with a life on *both* elements—sea and land.
(v) **anachronism**, an error in the placing of an event; as if we were to speak of railways as existing in the last century. The *chron* appears also in **chronology**, an account of time (or dates); **chronometer**, a *metron* (or measure) of time.

(vi) **anarchy**, a state of lawlessness. Gr. *archē*, rule. So **monarchy** is the rule of *one;* **oligarchy**, the rule of a *few*; **heptarchy**, *seven* kingdoms (or rules).

(vii) **anemoné**, the wind-flower. Gr. *anĕmos*, wind.

(viii) **antipathy** = a feeling against. The Gr. *anti* is also found in **antipodes** (= with feet against); **antithesis** (= a setting against); **antidote** (= something given against).

(ix) **archaic**, something *ancient.* Gr. *archaios*, old, or out of date.

(x) **archipelago**, the *chief* sea, or Ægean Sea. As the Ægean happened to be studded with islands, every sea full of islands come to be called an *archipelago.*

(xi) **arithmetic**, the science of number. Our Saxon forefathers called it *rime-craft*, *rime* being the Old English for number. So they called **astronomy**, *star-craft.*

LESSON 44.

athlete	caligraphy	chemist	democracy
autobiography	calomel	chronology	diagnosis
autograph	catarrh	chrysalis	diphtheria
banisters	catastrophé	cosmopolite	diphthong
barometer	catechise	decade	dynasty
botany	catholic	demagogue	encomium

(i) **autobiography**, a life of a person by himself. Gr. *autos*, self; *bios*, life; *graphé*, a description. The prefix *autos* is also found in **autograph** (= a paper written in one's *own* handwriting) ; **autonomy** (= self-rule); **automăton** (= a self-moving machine).

(ii) **barometer**, an instrument for measuring the weight of the air. Gr. *baros* (weight) and *metron* (a measure).

(iii) **caligraphy** = beautiful writing.

(iv) **catarrh** (= a "flowing down"), a bad cold. The Gr. *cata* is also found in **catastrophé**, a "turning down," or disaster.

(v) **catholic** = universal.

(vi) **cosmopolite** = an inhabitant of the world.

(vii) **decade** = a sum of ten years. The Gr. *deca* is also found in **decalogue** (= the ten commandments) ; **decagon** (= a ten-cornered figure).

Lesson 45.

encyclopædia	hierarchy	meteor	oxygen
entomology	hydropathy	mnemonics	pandemonium
ephemeral	hydrostatics	monotony	panorama
glycerine	kaleidoscope	narcotic	parenthesis
heptarchy	lithography	neuralgia	photography
heterodox	melodrama	ornithology	phrenology

(i) **encyclopædia**, the circle of arts and sciences. Gr. *kyklos* (a circle) and *paideia* (instruction).

(ii) **entomology**, the science of insects.

(iii) **ephemeral**, lasting only for a day.

(iv) **heterodox**, of an opinion *other* than the right. Opposed to **orthodox**.

(v) **hierarchy**, the rule of priests.

(vi) **hydropathy**, treatment of illness by water.

(vii) **lithography**, writing on stone.

(viii) **mnemonics**, the science of memory.

(ix) **neuralgia**, pain in the nerves.

(x) **photography**, writing with light. The Gr. *phos* (light) is also found in **phosphorus** (= light-bringer).

(xi) **phrenology** (= the "science of mind") has come to mean the science of the brain and its growth.

Lesson 46.

polemical	stereoscope	telephone	trigonometry
polyglot	stereotype	telescope	trophy
polysyllable	strychnine	theism	typhus
polygon	style	theology	zephyr
skeleton	tantalise	thermometer	zodiac
statics	telegraph	trisyllable	zone

(i) **polemical**, warlike (in writings). Gr. *polĕmos*, war.

(ii) **polyglot** = many-tongued. Gr. *polys* (many) is also found in **polysyllable**; **polypus** (= many-footed); **polytheism** (= a religion of many gods); **polygon** (= many-angled).

(iii) **stereoscope**, an instrument for showing "solid." The Gr. *stereos* (solid) is also found in **stereotype**.

(iv) **tantalise**, to tease. A Greek hero, Tantalus, was placed in Hades up to his chin in water; and, whenever he tried to drink, the water sank away.

(v) **telegraph**, a writer from a distance. The Gr. *telé* (far off) is found also in **telephone** (= a sounder or speaker from a distance); **telescope** (= a seer from a distance).
(vi) **thermometer**, a measurer of heat. Gr. *thermos*, heat.
(vii) **zone**, a belt.

19. **Slavonic Words.**—We have in our language a few words from the East of Europe—from Russian, Polish, Bohemian, Servian, etc., all of which are included under the term **Slav** or **Slavonic**. (This word also gives us the noun **slave**; as the Romans and Germans bought and brought their bond-servants from the East.) These few words chiefly relate to things found only in Eastern Europe.

LESSON 47.

calash	knout	rouble	vampire
drosky	morse	sable	verst
howitzer	polka	steppe	ukase

(i) **calash**, an open carriage.
(ii) **howitzer**, a short light cannon.
(iii) **knout**, the Russian cat-o'-nine-tails.
(iv) **morse**, a walrus.
(v) **rouble**, a coin worth 3s. 4d.
(vi) **steppe**, a wide plain.
(vii) **vampire**, a blood-sucker.
(viii) **verst**, a measure of 3500 feet.
(ix) **ukase**, an edict of the Czar.

20. **Persian Words.**—We have taken words from Persia; and, in most cases, the names came into this country along with the things, or they are the names of things which we first learned to know about in that country. A few of them came into our language by way of France. The following is a list of the more important.

Lesson 48.

asparagus	dervish	lime	satrap
bazaar	exchequer	magic	scarlet
caravan	jar	myrtle	scimitar
caravansary	jujube	orange	sepoy
carcase	laudanum	paradise	tiger
curry	lemon	rice	turkey

(i) **caravansary**, an inn for caravans (= company of travellers).
(ii) **curry**, a highly seasoned dish.
(iii) **dervish**, a Persian monk.
(iv) **exchequer** meant originally a *chess-board*; then the chequered cloth on which accounts were calculated by the aid of counters.
(v) **jar**, in the sense of *earthen pot*.
(vi) **lime**, in the sense of *citron*. Lime out of which mortar is made and **lime** (= linden-tree) are both purely English words.
(vii) **orange** was in Persian *naranj*. The n clung by mistake to the article, and *a naranj* became *an orange*. The same kind of mistake has been made in English: *a newt* became *an ewt* or *eft*.
(viii) **satrap** = Persian viceroy.
(ix) **sepoy** = a horseman, now applied to a native soldier in India.

21. **Words from Various Sources.**—There are very few parts of the world and very few peoples on the globe from which the English language has not borrowed words, and adopted them as her own children. The following are a few taken from the Hungarians and the Turks, both of which peoples—though living in Europe—are not Europeans at all, but Asiatics. Both are of Tartar race.

Lesson 49.

Hungarian Words.	Turkish Words.	
hussar	bey	janizary
sabre	caftan	ottoman
shako	caviare	shagreen
tokay	chouse	uhlan

(i) **hussar**, a light cavalry soldier.
(ii) **sabre**, a kind of scimitar.
(iii) **shako**, a kind of military hat.

(iv) **tokay**, the fine wine grown on the southern slopes of the Carpathians round the town of Tokay.
(v) **bey**, a governor of a province.
(vi) **caftan**, a long vest tied round the waist with a girdle.
(vii) **caviare**, the roe of the sturgeon.
(viii) **chouse**, to cheat.
(ix) **janizary**, a soldier of the old Turkish foot-guard.
(x) **ottoman**, a low stuffed seat, called after Othman, the founder of the Ottoman (or Turkish) Empire.
(xi) **shagreen**, a rough-grained leather; or shark's skin.
(xii) **uhlan**, a light cavalry (lancers), used much by the Germans for rapid movements in the Franco-German war of 1871.

22. Sanscrit Words.—Sanscrit is the oldest language in the world. It is a *dead* language; that is, it is no longer *spoken* by any people. It is the language of the holy books of the Hindoo priests. It is, moreover, the language from which almost all the languages of Europe and Asia have sprung; it is the root of them all. The following are the most important words we have borrowed from it.

LESSON 50.

banyan	indigo	mandarin	rajah
brahmin	jungle	muscatel	rupee
brilliant	lac	musk	saccharine
chintz	lacquer	punch	sandal
crimson	loot	pundit	sugar
ginger	mace	punkah	suttee

(i) **banyan**, an Indian fig-tree, the branches of which send down shoots which grow into roots, enlarge into trunks, and themselves send out branches. On the banks of the Nerbudda is a banyan-tree with 3500 trunks. It has been known to shelter 7000 men.
(ii) **brahmin** (or **brahman**), a person of the upper and sacred caste among the Hindoos.
(iii) **lac** has two meanings: (*a*) a resin produced on the banyan-tree by a small insect—from this comes **lacquer**; (*b*) a hundred thousand—"a lac of rupees."
(iv) **loot**=plunder or booty. It is also used as a verb.
(v) **mace**, in the sense of *spice*. (**Mace**=club, is of French origin.) Mace is the dried covering of the seed of the nutmeg.
(vi) **muscatel**, a wine with a flavour of **musk**.

(vii) **punch,** in the sense of a drink composed of *five* ingredients. The same word is found (with a slightly different spelling) in **Punjab** = the land of the *five* rivers.
(viii) **pundit** = a learned man.
(ix) **punkah** = a large fan, generally driven by a wheel.
(x) **rajah** = king. *Raj* is the same word as *reg* in *regal*. **Maharajah** (= mag-nus rex) means *emperor*.
(xi) **suttee** = the burning of a widow on the funeral pile of her husband.

23. **Arabic Words.**—We have borrowed, and retained, from the Arabs a considerable number of words. Most of these are the names of things with which the Arabs first made us acquainted. It must not be forgotten that the Arabs were for many hundreds of years the strongest power on the Mediterranean; and that their empire at one time extended from the Pyrenees to the Himalayas, and from Lisbon to Samarcand. The following are some of the most important words which they have contributed to our language. A large number have come to us through Spanish; and a few through French.

Lesson 51.

alcove	amulet	emir	minaret
algebra	arsenal	hookah	Moslem
alkali	attar	howdah	mosque
alkoran	azure	jerboa	muezzin
albatross	dragoman	magazine	mufti
amber	elixir	masquerade	myrrh

(i) **alcove,** a recess. (The *al* is the Arabic definite article.) This word has no connection with the English word *cove*.
(ii) **algebra** = *the* art of calculating by letters or symbols.
(iii) **alkali** = *the* salt (*kali* was the name given to the ashes of a plant).
(iv) **alkoran** = *the* Koran, the sacred book of the Mahometans.
(v) **amulet,** a charm against evil. (Literally, "a thing carried.")
(vi) **attar** = perfumed oil or essential oil (of roses).
(vii) **dragoman,** an interpreter. The word was brought to England by the Crusaders.
(viii) **elixir,** an essence. (Literally, "the philosopher's stone," the touch of which turned a thing to gold. *El* is another form of *al*.)

(ix) **emir**, a commander or prince. In Afghanistan it is spelt **Ameer**. Another form of it is found in **admiral**, which in Old English was spelt **amiral**.

(x) **hookah**, a pipe with a long pliable tube, the smoke from which passes through water.

(xi) **howdah**, the seat on an elephant's back.

(xii) **jerboa**, a small rodent, of about the size of a cat.

(xiii) **minaret**, a turret on a mosque.

(xiv) **muezzin**, the Mahometan officer who calls the faithful to prayers from a minaret.

(xv) **mufti**, a magistrate. But the phrase "in mufti" has come to mean in civilian costume (as opposed to military uniform).

LESSON 52.

mate	Mussulman	saffron	syrup
mattress	naphtha	senna	tariff
mohair	nabob	sirocco	tartar
monsoon	nitre	sultan	zenith

(i) **mate**, in the sense of *to confound* or *kill*. The phrase **check-mate** is = the king is dead = *sheikh mat*; or, in Persian, *Shah mat*. (The English word **mate** is connected with *meet*.)

(ii) **mohair**, cloth made of the hair of the Angora goat.

(iii) **monsoon**, a season wind.

(iv) **Mussulman**, a true believer. The shorter form is **Moslem**.

(v) **nitre**, another name for saltpetre. The chief use is to make gunpowder.

(vi) **nabob**, an Indian prince, a very rich man. (Literally, a viceroy.) The most correct spelling is **Nawab**.

(vii) **sirocco**, a hot wind from Africa.

(viii) **tartar**, an acid salt.

(ix) **zenith**, the "top of the sky"—the part right overhead. The opposite part is called the **nadir**.

24. Hebrew Words.—We have in our language a number of Hebrew words, which we received at different periods. Some were brought into England by the monks who came with Augustine in the sixth century; others we learnt from the Bible; others were introduced by travellers. The following words are the most important.

Lesson 53.

abbot	cider	jockey	Pharisee
abbess	cinnamon	jubilee	Sadducee
abbey	damask	leviathan	sapphire
amen	elephant	Mammon	seraph
cab	gauze	manna	shekel
camel	hallelujah	maudlin	shibboleth

(i) **abbot**, the father or head of an abbey. Heb. *abba*, father.
(ii) **amen** = so let it be!
(iii) **damask**, from Damascus, a city in Syria.
(iv) **gauze**, from Gaza, a city in Palestine.
(v) **hallelujah** = Praise ye Jah (Jehovah)!
(vi) **Mammon**, the Syrian god of riches. Milton says of him:

> Mammon, the least erected spirit that fell
> From heaven; for even in heaven his looks and thoughts
> Were always downward bent, admiring more
> The riches of heaven's pavement, trodden gold,
> Than aught divine or holy.

(vii) **manna**, the food sent to the Israelites in the wilderness of Arabia.
(viii) **maudlin**, a corruption of *Magdalen*. The original sense was "shedding tears of penitence."
(ix) **sapphire**, a precious blue stone.
(x) **shibboleth**, the test-word of a party. See Judges xii. 6.

25. **Asiatic Words.**—These words have come into our language from Hindostan, Malaysia, China, and other parts of the East. They are mostly names of things that exist in these countries, or that have been imported from them into Great Britain. The following words are the most important.

Lesson 54.

HINDOSTANI.		FROM MALAY, CHINA, etc.	
bonnet	shampoo	bamboo	nankeen
bungalow	teak	cassowary	orang-outang
calico	thug	cockatoo	sago
coolie	toddy	gutta-percha	silk
cowry	tulip	japan	tea
rum	turban	junk	typhoon

(i) **bungalow**, a Bengal thatched house.

(ii) **calico**, cotton cloth named from Calicut, on the west or Malabar coast of India.
(iii) **coolie**, an East Indian porter.
(iv) **cowry**, a small shell used for money. The word was also carried to the Guinea Coast, in Africa.
(v) **thug**, a member of a secret religious body in India who used to murder travellers.
(vi) **toddy**, the juice of the palmyra tree, now applied to a mixture of spirits and hot water.
(vii) **junk**, a Chinese three-masted vessel.
(viii) **nankeen**, a kind of cotton cloth called after **Nankin** (=North Court), the old capital of China.
(ix) **typhoon** (= "great wind"), a violent hurricane in the China seas.

26. **American-Indian Words.**—These words come to us from both the Americas; and they are mostly names of things and animals that belong to these continents. The following is an almost complete list.

LESSON 55.

alpaca	guano	maize	quinine
buccaneer	hominy	mocassin	squaw
cacao	hurricane	opossum	tapioca
cannibal	ipecacuanha	pampa	tapir
canoe	jaguar	peccary	tobacco
chocolate	llama	potato	tomahawk

(i) **alpaca**, the long-haired "sheep" of Peru. It belongs to the camel tribe, and is a small variety of the **llama**.
(ii) **buccaneer**, a kind of pirate. A West Indian word.
(iii) **cacao** (wrongly called **cocoa**), a tree which produces the seeds from which **chocolate** is made. Both words are Mexican.
(iv) **canoe**, a West Indian name for *boat*.
(v) **guano**, a Peruvian word for the dung of sea-fowls.
(vi) **hominy**, maize cooked. West Indian.
(vii) **ipecacuanha** (called also shortly **ipec**) is a West Indian name for a plant. (The word is = "the sick-making plant.")
(viii) **maize** = Indian corn. West Indian word.
(ix) **mocassin**, a shoe of deer-skin. North American.
(x) **opossum**, the only marsupial (= pouched animal) in America.
(xi) **pampas**, wide plains in the south of South America.

(xii) **peccary**, the wild hog of South America.
(xiii) **potato**. Name and thing were brought to England from South America in 1563 by Sir John Hawkins.
(xiv) **quinine**, or "Peruvian bark," is the extract of the cinchona tree. Name and thing came from Peru.
(xv) **squaw**, a wife. West Indian.
(xvi) **tapir**, the small "elephant" of South America. The tapir is allied to the hog and to the rhinoceros.
(xvii) **tomahawk**, a light war-hatchet. West Indian.

27. **African Words.**—African travel has given us a number of words; but they mostly relate to things and animals which are found in that continent. The following is a list of the most important words.

Lesson 56.

baobab	fustian	guinea	papyrus
barb	gnu	ibis	quagga
barge	giraffe	morocco	sack
canary	gorilla	oasis	satchel
chimpanzee	gypsy	paper	zebra

(i) **baobab** (or "monkey-bread tree") is one of the largest trees in the world. It is sometimes 30 feet in diameter. The name comes from Senegal.
(ii) **barb**, shortened from Barbary (horse).
(iii) **canary**, a bird from the Canary Islands, off the coast of Africa.
(iv) **chimpanzee**, a large ape of West Africa.
(v) **gnu**, a kind of antelope found in South Africa. A Hottentot word.
(vi) **gorilla**, a very large ape, found in the equatorial forests of Africa.
(vii) **gypsy**, a corruption of *Gyptian*—a contraction of *Egyptian*.
(viii) **guinea**, originally gold from the coast of Guinea.
(ix) **ibis**, an Egyptian wading-bird, to which divine honours were paid.
(x) **morocco**, a kind of leather prepared (at first) by the Moors of Morocco.
(xi) **oasis**, a fertile spot in a desert. A Libyan word.
(xii) **papyrus**, the Nile reed from which **paper** (name and thing) was first made.
(xiii) **quagga**, an animal allied to the zebra, and found on the plains of South Africa. A Hottentot word.
(xiv) **sack**, a bag. See Genesis xxxvii. 34. Dim. **satchel**.
(xv) **zebra**, a striped animal of the horse kind, found in South Africa.

PART X

THE THOUSAND MOST DIFFICULT WORDS
IN THE ENGLISH LANGUAGE
SELECTED FROM EXAMINATION PAPERS

Abbreviation	bb	aggrieved	gg-ie	antithesis	thes
abeyance	ey	aghast	gha	anxiety	ie
abridgment	dgm	agreeable	ee	Apennines	penn
abscess	sc	aide-de-camp	aide	aperient	eri
abyss	yss	aisle	ais	apostasy	asy
academician	ici	algebraical	rai	apothecary	eca
accede	ede	alien	ie	appalling	all
accelerate	cc-l-r	allegiance	egi	appellation	pp-ll
accessible	ible	alligator	lig	appetite	et
accommodate	cc-mm	amanuensis	m	appraise	pp
accountant	ant	amass	m-ss	appreciable	eci
accumulate	cc-m	amateur	at-eu	appurtenance	ppur
achievement	ie-e	ambassador	ssad	aquarium	qu
acknowledgment	dgm	ameliorate	elior	aqueduct	ue
acquiesce	iesce	amenable	men	aquiline	uil
acreage	eage	amethyst	eth	archiepiscopal	ie
acrimonious	rim	amiability	bili	archipelago	pela
address	dd-ss	ammunition	iti	argosy	gos
adequacy	acy	amnesty	est	aristocratic	atic
admissible	ssib	analogous	al	arithmetician	cian
adolescence	sce	ancient	cie	armament	mam
advantageous	geo	animalcula (*pl.*)	cul	arraign	rr-gn
aerial	ri	ankle	kle	arrears	rr
aeronaut	ron	annals	nn	artesian	esi
affability	ff	annuitant	ant	articulate	cul
affright	ff	anomalous	nom	artificial	ici
affront	ff	anonymous	nym	artillery	iller
afraid	f	Antarctic	rc	ascetic	scet
aggravate	av	antediluvian	dil	asinine	in-ine
aggregate	reg	antiquary	ary	asparagus	para

assassin	ss-ss	battalion	tt	buccaneer	neer
assessment	ss-ss	bayonet	yon	buoy	uo
assiduous	uous	bazaar	aar	buoyant	ant
assuage	ua	beau-idéal	eal	burlesque	sque
asterisk	ter	beauteous	eous	buttress	tt-ss
astronomer	ono	beginning	nn	buzzard	zz
atheism	the	beguile	gui	by-and-by	y-y
atrocious	oci	behaviour	vi		
attorney	tor	beleaguer	uer		
auburn	au	belfry	lf		
audacious	aci	believe	ieve	Cabal	al
auger (a tool)	er	belligerent	ent	cabinet	net
augur (a person)	ur	benefice	ne	caitiff	ff
auricular	ic	bequeath	uea	calamitous	mit
auriferous	ifer	beseech	ee	calculus	ulus
auxiliary	ilia	besiege	ie	calendar	ar
average	age	biassed	ss	calomel	omel
aviary	vi	bicycle	cyc	camelopard	lop
avoirdupois	oirdu	biennial	nn	campaign	aign
awkward	wk	bigamy	gam	cancelled	ll
awry	wr	billiards	lli	cannonade	nnon
		biscuit	ui	canonical	al
		bivouac	ouac	canteen	een
		blamable	ma	caoutchouc	ou-ouc
		bludgeon	geon	capability	bil
		boatswain	ain	capillary	ary
		borough	ough	caricature	rica
		boudoir	oir	carriage	rria
		boulder	oul	cartilage	til
		boulevard	lev	cashier	ier
Bacchanalian	ana	bouquet	uet	castellated	ll
bagatelle	gat	braggart	gg	catalogue	tal
banditti	tt	breeches	ee	catarrh	arrh
bankruptcy	tcy	breviary	via	category	ory
bargain	gain	brilliancy	lli	cavalier	ier
barometer	met	Britanny	nn	cavilling	ll
baronetcy	tcy	bronchitis	ch	cede	ede
barracks	rra	brougham	ough	ceiling	ei
barrenness	nn	bruise	ui	celery	ery
barricade	rric	brusque	sque	centaur	aur

June.

centenary	ten	confectionery	ery	Dandelion	deli
cereal	re	confederacy	acy	decalogue	cal
chamberlain	ain	conferred	rr	decapitate	pit
chameleon	ele	connoisseur	oiss	deceive	ei
champagne	agne	conscientious	ent	deciduous	uous
chargeable	ge	consequential	tial	deferred	rr
charlatan	lat	conservative	ive	deficient	ent
chateau	eau	constabulary	bul	deign	ei
chemical	mic	constituency	titu	delicacy	acy
cheque	eque	consummate	mm	delicious	ici
chestnut	tn	contemporary	ary	demagogue	mag
chieftain	ie-ai	contour	our	derivative	ive
chilblain	lb-ai	contraband	tra	descendant	ant
chimneys	eys	contrariwise	ri	despondent	ent
chivalry	lry	contumely	ely	despotically	ally
cigarette	ette	convalescence	esc	desuetude	suet
cinnamon	nn	convivial	ivi	deteriorate	eri
circuitous	ous	coquette	ette	detriment	tri
citadel	tad	coralline	ll	development	opm
citizen	tiz	corduroy	uroy	dexterous	ous
civilian	lian	corollary	lla	dialogue	logue
clique	ique	corridor	idor	dictionary	ary
coalesce	esce	cortege	ege	dietary	ary
cochineal	chin	coterie	rie	dignitary	ary
cocoa	oa	councillor	illor	dilapidate	di
coefficient	fici	counterfeit	ei	diocese	ese
coincidence	ence	courier	ier	diphthong	phth
collateral	ll-t	courteous	eous	disadvantageous	eous
colleague	ea	credibility	bili	disagreeable	ee
colliery	ery	crescent	sc	disappoint	s-pp
colloquial	oqui	cruise	ui	disarrangement	ge
colonel	lon	crystalline	all	disbelieve	ie
commensurate	mm	cuirass	cui	discernible	ible
commiserate	miser	cuneiform	ei	discoloration	lor
commodious	mm	curlew	lew	discriminate	crim
comparative	rat	curriculum	cul	disguise	gui
compatibility	tibi	curtsey	sey	dishabille	ille
competitive	tit	customary	ary	disinfectant	ant
conceit	ei	cyclopedia	oped	disobedient	dis
concurrence	rr			disparagement	age

L

dispossess	ss-ss	epistolary	ola	feudalism	lism
dissatisfaction	diss	equally	lly	fictitious	titi
disseminate	min	equanimity	imi	fiendish	ie
dissipation	ssip	equerry	rry	filibuster	ili
dissyllable	diss	equilateral	ter	flageolet	eo
doggerel	ger	equivalent	val	flippancy	ancy
domain	ain	era	e	floe (of ice)	oe
domicile	icile	erysipelas	rys	foreign	eign
donkey	key	eschew	ch	forfeit	feit
doughty	ought	escutcheon	eon	fortuitous	ui
driveller	ll	ethereal	eal	foully	lly
dryly	yly	evenness	nn	fratricide	trici
dudgeon	geon	exaggerate	gg	fraudulent	ul
duellist	ll	exasperate	per	freight	ei
dulness	l	exceed	ee	frieze	ie
dungeon	geon	exchequer	uer	frolicking	ck
dysentery	ery	excrescence	sc	frolicsome	cs
		exhilarate	hil	frontispiece	ie
		expedition	di	fusilier	ier
		exquisite	quis		
ECCENTRIC	cc	extinct	nct	GAILY	ai
ecstasy	asy	extraordinarily	ar	gaiety	ety
effeminacy	ff	extravagance	rava	galleon	eon
efficient	ici	eyry	ey	gambolling	ll
eighth	hth			gaoler	er
electrician	ici			garrison	rris
eleemosynary	ee-syn-ary			gaseous	eous
eligibility	bili			gauntlet	au
embarrassment	rr-ss			gazetteer	tteer
embodiment	di			gherkin	gh
emigrate	ig	FACILITATE	ili	giraffe	affe
emphasis	pha	factitious	titi	gladiator	ia
encyclopedia	cyc-ped	fallacious	ll	glutinous	tin
ennoble	nn	fanaticism	tic	gorgeous	eous
entail	en	farinaceous	in-ace	gourmand	our
enthusiast	thu	fascinate	sci	gradient	ient
envelope (*n.*)	ope	fatiguing	uing	graminivorous	mini
epaulet	au	fatuity	uity	granary	ary
epigrammatic	mm	feign	ei	graphic	ph
episcopacy	acy	ferrule (a metal ring)	rr	gratuity	ui

IN THE ENGLISH LANGUAGE 147

grenadier	na	impropriety	pri	inutility	ility
grievance	iev	impugn	ugn	inveigh	eigh
guarantee	ua	inaccessible	cc-ss	inveigle	eig
guerilla	ue	inalienable	lie	ipecacuanha	anha
guillotine	ll	inappreciable	pp-ci	irascible	sc
guinea	ui-ea	inaugurate	gur	irrefragable	rag
gunwale	wale	incendiary	iary	irrigate	rig
guttural	ur	incommensurable	mm	isosceles	osc
		incommode	mm	isthmus	sth
		incomparable	par	itinerant	itin
Hackneyed	ey	incompatibility	tibi	itinerary	er
hammock	mm	inconsistency	ency		
harangue	gue	incurred	rr		
harass	r-ss	indefeasible	ea		
harlequin	le	indictment	ctm		
haughtiness	ti	indivisible	ible		
heifer	ei	indomitable	mit		
heinous	ei	inflexible	ible		
hereditary	dit	influenza	enz		
hiccough	cc	ingenious	geni		
honorary	or	ingenuous	genu	Janitor	nit
hurricane	rri	initial	iti	January	ua
hydropathic	ic	initiatory	ory	japanned	nn
		inquisitor	or	jargonelle	elle
		insatiable	atia	jaundice	au
		insignia	nia	jeopardy	ardy
		insistence	ence	jeweller	ll
		insolubility	ubil	judicial	dici
		instability	stab	jugglery	ery
		integer	eger	jugular	gul
Icicle	cle	integument	tegu	justiciary	ici
idolatrous	tr	intelligibility	bili		
igneous	ne	interchangeable	ge		
illiterate	iter	intermittent	tt		
immigrant	mmig	internecine	nec		
immovable	mm	interrogative	gat		
impatience	ti	intricacy	acy		
impossibility	bili	intrigue	igue		
impressible	ible	intrinsically	ally		
improbability	bili	intuitive	ive		

Kaleidoscope	ei	literature	tera	mathematician	cian
kerchief	ie	litigious	igi	matrimonial	trim
khedive	khe	lodestone	ode	Mauritius	tius
		logician	cian	mechanically	ally
		longevity	evi	medicinally	lly
		loquacious	ious	Mediterranean	terr
		lugubrious	ubr	meerschaum	sch
		luminary	ary	memorial	rial
		luncheon	eon	menacing	cing
		luscious	sci	menagerie	erie
Laboratory	rat	lyrical	ical	mercenary	ary
lachrymose	chry			meridian	idi
lackey	ey			metaphysician	cian
lacquer	cqu			meteor	ete
languor	uor			meteorology	olo
lapidary	pid			methodically	ally
larceny	eny			mignonette	gno
laudatory	ory			millennium	ll
lavatory	vat			mimicking	ck
league	gue			minaret	ar
lectern (a stand for reading)	ern	**Mackerel**	cker	miniature	ia
legendary	ary	magician	cian	minutiæ	iæ
legible	gi	magnanimous	nan	misbelieve	ie
leisure	ei	mahogany	any	miscellaneous	ane
leopard	eo	maintenance	ten	mischievous	iev
lettuce	tt	malicious	ious	misgiving	s
levelled	ll	manacle	nac	mislaid	s
leveret	eret	manœuvre	œu	misshapen	ss
libellous	ll	mantelpiece	tel	missile	ss
librarian	br	marauder	au	missionary	ary
lichen	chen	marchioness	chi	misstate	ss
liege	ie	marionette	ette	mistake	s
lieutenant	ant	maritime	iti	mitigate	iti
liliputian	lili	marriageable	age	mitre	tre
limn	mn	marshalled	all	mnemonics	mne
lineage	ea	martinet	tin	modelling	ll
liniment	ni	marvellous	ell	moiety	oi
liqueur	ueur	masquerade	quer	molasses	ass
liquorice	ice	massacre	acre	momentarily	ri
literally	ll	materially	lly	monosyllabic	mono

IN THE ENGLISH LANGUAGE 149

monotonous	noto	OBEISANCE	ei	paralysis	lys
morass	rass	obituary	itu	parliament	ia
moreover	more	obsequies	quies	parricide	rri
morocco	occ	occasionally	ally	participial	ipial
mosquito	qui	occurrence	rr	patriarch	tri
mountainous	ai	octogenarian	gen	patrician	cian
moustache	ache	oculist	cul	patrolling	ll
movable	va	offertory	ory	patronymic	nym
mulct	lct	official	cial	pavilion	ili
mummery	ery	ominous	min	peasantry	ant
munificence	cence	omitted	tt	peccadillo	cc
murrain	rr	omniscience	ence	peculiarity	ity
musician	cian	onerous	er	pedagogue	da
Mussulman	sul	oppressor	or	pedigree	dig
mutability	bili	optician	cian	pendant (flag)	ant
mutiny	iny	oracular	cul	penitentiary	ary
		ordinance	ance	Pentateuch	eu
		ordnance	dn	peremptorily	empt
		orifice	if	permissible	ible
		originally	ally	persecutor	or
NAPHTHA	phth	oscillating	ill	petroleum	ole
nauseous	eous	osseous	ss	pettifogger	gg
naval (adj.)	al	outrageous	eous	phaeton	ae
necessarily	ar	overreach	rr	pharisaical	ai
nectarine	ine	oxidise	dise	phenomenon	men
negligent	lig			philippic	pp
nicotine	cot			phthisis	phth
nitrogen	ro			physician	cian
nominative	ive			physiognomy	nom
non-commissioned	mm-ss			pillory	ory
nonpareil	eil	PÆAN	æ	pinion	ion
noticeable	tice	pageant	age	piquant	qu
nucleus	cle	palatable	able	pistil (of a flower)	il
nugget	gg	pallor	or	plaguy	uy
nuisance	ui	pamphleteer	eer	plaice (a fish)	ai
numerical	ric	panacea	cea	plaintiff	iff
nutritive	ive	pandemonium	dem	plebeian	ei
		panegyric	egyr	plebiscite	isc
		parachute	a	plenipotentiary	iary
		parallel	all	pleurisy	eu

THE THOUSAND MOST DIFFICULT WORDS

pneumatic	pneu	prosiness	si	receipt	ei
politician	cian	provincial	cial	receiver	er
polysyllable	syll	prowess	ess	recipé	ipe
pomegranate	meg	psychology	psy	reciprocity	ity
pontifical	ific	ptarmigan	pt	reconnoitre	oi
porcelain	cel	pulley	ey	recriminate	crim
Portuguese	guese	pumice	ice	recruit	uit
possess	ss-ss	purlieu	ieu	reducible	ible
postilion	til	pursuivant	suiv	regatta	atta
potable	able	purvey	ey	regrettable	able
potentate	ate	putrefy	re	re-issue	iss
poultice	ou	pygmy	pyg	re-iterate	iter
practitioner	tit	Pyrenees	r-n	release	ea
prairie	ai-ie			reliable	li
prebendary	ary			relief	ief
pre-eminent	e-e			remediless	i
preferred	erred			removable	able
preliminary	limi			renunciation	un
preoccupy	occ			repository	tory
preparatory	tory			repressible	ible
prerogative	roga	Quadrilateral	lat	reprieve	ie
presbytery	byt	quarrelling	ll	requiem	qui
presentiment	ti	quay	uay	research	ea
principal (a person)	pal	query	ery	reservoir	oir
principle	ple	queue	eue	resistible	ible
privilege	ege	quotient	ient	restaurant	au
proboscis	osc			resurrection	rr
proceed	eed			reticule	tic
procedure	ed			retrieve	ie
producible	ible			reynard	
proficient	fici	Rabbinical	nic	rhetorician	ician
progenitor	nit	raillery	ll	rhyme	rhy
prohibitory	ory	rancorous	cor	righteous	eous
prologue	ogue	rapacious	ious	rime (hoar-frost)	ri
promissory	iss	rarefy	e	role (a part in a play)	ole
pronunciation	un	rarity	i	rosary	sary
proprietary	ary	reactionary	ary	rueful	ue
propriety	pri	really	ll	ruminate	min
prorogue	ogue	rebellious	ious		
proselyte	lyte	recapitulatory	ory		

IN THE ENGLISH LANGUAGE 151

Saccharine	cch	shield	ie	subsidiary		idi
sacrificial	fici	shriek	ie	succeed		ceed
salary	lary	shyly	y	succulent		cc
saleable	le	siege	ie	suddenness		nn
saltpetre	etre	Sikh	ikh	sufficient		ient
sanguinary	nary	similar	mil	suffragan		frag
sapphire	pp	singeing	ge	suicide		ui
satiety	ety	sleight	ei	summarily		ari
satire (a poem)	ire	sluice	ui	sumptuary		ary
satyr	yr	soldiery	iery	superficies		fici
saucily	i	solicitor	or	supersede		ede
savagery	ery	soliloquy	oquy	superstitious		tious
saviour	iour	soporific	por	suppress		pp
scalable	la	sortie	tie	supremacy		acy
scarlatina	lat	souvenir	nir	surfeit		eit
sciatica	sci	sovereign	sov	surgeon		geon
scimitar	sc-ar	spaniel	nie	surplice		ice
scintillate	ill	spectacle	acle	surrender		rr
scrofulous	ous	spermaceti	cet	surreptitious		pti
scrupulous	pul	spontaneous	eous	surveillance		eill
scrutinise	ise	sprightliness	li	susceptibility		bili
scutcheon	eon	squadron	ron	sycamore		syc
scythe	scy	squalor	lor	sycophant		syco
secede	ede	squirearchy	ire	sylvan		syl
secession	ess	squirrel	rr	symmetry		mm
secretary	ary	starveling	ve	symphony		phon
sedentary	ary	stationary	ary	synagogue		syn
sediment	i	stationery (paper, etc.)	ery	synonym		non
Seine	ei	statistician	cian	synthesis		thes
sempstress	pst	statutory	tory	syrup		syr
sentiment	ti	stereotype	ereo	Tabour		our
separate	par	stirrup	rr	tactician		ician
septuagenarian	gen	stoicism	cism	talisman		lis
sequel	quel	stomachic	ach	tankard		ard
seraglio	agl	storey (in a house)	ey	tarpaulin		au
sergeant (in the army)	ge	stratagem	ata	tasselled		ll
serviceable	ice	strategy	egy	tattooing		oo
sexagenarian	agen	strychnine	ych	tautological		olog
shagreen	ee	sturgeon	eon	tawdrily		i
sheik	ei	subpœna	œ	technical		ech

telegram	tele	typography	typ	verdigris	dig
tenacious	ious	tyranny	nn	verisimilitude	4 i's
tenement	tene			vermicelli	mic
tesselated	ss			vermilion	ili
theologian	gi			vertebrate	teb
thews	ews			veterinary	ary
thief	ie			vicegerent	vice
throe	oe			vicissitude	ss
thyme	thy			victuals	uals
tidily	i			vignette	gn
tingeing	geing	Ukase	ase	villainy	ain
tissue	ue	ultramarine	a	vitreous	tre
tonsils	ils	umbrageous	eous	vizier	ier
torpor	or	unabbreviated	bb	vocabulary	abul
tortoise	oi	unaccommodating	cc-mm	volunteer	eer
totally	ll	unappreciated	pp	vouchsafe	safe
tournament	na	unbiassed	ss		
towelling	ll	unchangeable	ge		
traceable	ace	unembarrassed	rr-ss		
trafficking	ff	unfeigned	ei		
tragedian	ian	unguent	guent	Waggonette	ette
transcendent	ent	unintelligible	ll	wainscot	scot
trapeze	eze	unmanageable	age	walrus	l
treble	eble	unpronounceable	ce	weird	ei
tremor	or	unsavoury	oury	wharves	ves
trenchant	ant	unveil	ei	whereas	ere
triangular	gul	unwieldy	ie	whirligig	rl
tricycle	cyc			widgeon	eon
triennial	nn			wiseacre	se
triphthong	phth			witticism	tt
trisyllable	tris	Vacillate	ll	wooer	ooer
troubadour	our	valetudinarian	din		
trousseau	sseau	valise	ise	Yacht	acht
truculent	cul	valorous	or	yeoman	eo
truncheon	eon	variegated	ie	yield	ie
tumefaction	me	vassalage	al		
tunnelling	ll	vedette	ved		
turquoise	oise	vegetable	get	Zephyr	phyr
twelfth	lfth	velocipede	loci	zodiac	diac
typhoon	oon	vendor	or	zoology	oo

www.ingramcontent.com/pod-product-compliance
Lightning Source LLC
Chambersburg PA
CBHW030301170426
43202CB00009B/833